MEMOIRS OF A LECHUGUERO

Lucio Padilla

authorHOUSE®

AuthorHouse™
1663 Liberty Drive, Suite 200
Bloomington, IN 47403
www.authorhouse.com
Phone: 1-800-839-8640

This book is a work of non-fiction. Unless otherwise noted, the author and the publisher make no explicit guarantees as to the accuracy of the information contained in this book and in some cases, names of people and places have been altered to protect their privacy.

ISBN: 978-1-4343-2892-2 (sc)

First published by AuthorHouse 9/28/2007

Printed in the United States of America
Bloomington, Indiana
This book is printed on acid-free paper.

Dedication

I dedicate this book to María Elena who has been my companion in good times as well as bad. Her love and support have given me the inspiration and determination to overcome the hardships of life. I am fortunate to be with her to enjoy the fruits of our efforts.

My gratitude to Korina Rioseco Tabarez for her support in the development of this book.

"The more challenging a goal is, the more rewarding its accomplishment."

"Love is the best motivator to face the hardships of life."

"It's uncertain how far I can go; if I don't try I will never know."

By Lucio Padilla

Table of Contents

MY CRISIS

THE PAIN WAS TERRIBLE. My face reflected the agony I felt in my body and my soul. Containing a moan, I began to walk to the end of the field. The intense pain running down my leg worried me. I had not felt anything like it before. It was bad news and a sign of an uncertain future. I tried my best to conceal my worries, but despite my efforts my brother Rafael sensed something was wrong. He approached me and concerned, asked,

"*Órale homes* are you OK?"

"*Simón*," I answered, faking a smile that must have looked grim. "I am OK," I told my brother.

But Rafael was not fooled; he knew if I complained it had to be serious. I approached the foreman to report my injury.

"*Oye homes*, my leg hurts. I think I injured myself. I slipped earlier in the day and felt a muscle sprain. I worked with pain all day long," I explained.

The foreman listened with a serious expression. "Hey, you are OK," he said trying to dismiss me. "You are our best *lechuguero*[1]. You are always tough. I think it is just a sprained muscle and all you need is a

---

[1] Lettuce harvester

1

rub down." y rotar hacia abajo

"Look man," I said in dismay trying to control my anger, "I don't want consternación a massage, I am reporting an injury and if I don't feel better by tomorrow I want to go to the doctor."

I asked him for information to submit a workman's compensation claim. We argued about the injury. He insisted I had not shown any signs all day long. I worked hard as usual ahead of everybody, cutting and packing faster than any *lechuguero* in the crew. He hesitated but said vuelto he would give me the information the next day.

"I hope you are not faking," he said, and showing little concern, he left.

I saw him walk away, amazed at his change of attitude towards me. Since I started working for him he had praised my ability to do the alababa work. Now he ignored my pain with indifference and dismissed me like a disposable item.

The ninety-mile trip back to Calexico was very quiet. We were all tired and thirsty but more than anything my brother and friends respected my agony and limited their conversations. Rafael, el Poncho, el Johnny, my *Compas*[2] *Yuca y Chicho* and I, had worked together many seasons and had survived many ordeals. We were all in a precarious economic situation after four years of crop devastation by the white fly in Imperial Valley. Unemployment was high and those who were fortunate to have a stable job did not earn enough to save for the harsh summer. We were duro three days away from our first paycheck. It would be a decent check that would bring relief, but for now we were down to our last dollar. We did not have enough money to buy gas for the next day or to buy some refreshments for the two-hour drive. We were wet, cold, and broke but no one complained. We acted with pride refusing to display weakness Se quejo debilidad

---

[2] Godfather of one's child

and always had faith in finding a solution. I left my brother and *Compa Yuca* in Calipatria thirty miles north of Calexico. We picked them up daily on our way to Coachella. Half an hour later I left Johnny, Chicho and Poncho at the border. They lived in Mexicali[3] and crossed every day to work. As soon as I was alone I let go a long contained moan. The pain drilling my left leg was unbearable. I thought about buying a beer. Maybe a beer would ease my pain and help me to sleep. I only had three dollars left and needed money for gas the next day. It would take most of my money to buy it but I was desperate. I stopped at an AM-PM near my house and limped in the store. My toes were num and I was having difficulty raising my toes as I stepped, causing an uncontrollable limp. I was horrified at the thought of becoming crippled. I had seen many *lechugueros* young and old crippled by the demanding job. I had never thought it would ever happen to me. I felt so strong the day before. It was ironic how I joined other young *lechugueros* to harass the older or crippled workers calling them *guevones*[4] because they could not keep up to the younger harvesters. The old *lechugueros* responded aggressively using a great variety of insults.

"Así como te ves me vi y como me veo te veras[5]," they said with sarcasm.

I never thought it would come so soon. I entered the store and bought a *caguama*[6]. "This will help me with the pain," I kept telling myself. I wanted to believe that the *caguama* would heal my injury. I was desperate to get home and have a long drink of beer. But adding to my bad luck, as I limped towards the car, I stumbled and dropped

---

[3] City that borders with Calexico California

[4] Lazy

[5] The way you look I used to be, the way I am you will become.

[6] Quart of beer

the *caguama* shattering it as it hit the pavement of the parking lot. I could not believe my bad luck. I looked up at the sky in protest for my misfortune. I sadly saw the magic liquid spill on the floor. In despair, I let out a moan in disbelief of my tragedy.

The next day Chicho, Poncho, Johnny and I met at the usual reunion point. We all had failed to borrow money. I did not even try. The pain in my leg had been terrible and I hardly slept all night.

"*Nomás cinco mendigos dólares[7],*" Poncho said laughing and showing the five dollars we had together.

We hoped Rafael y mi *compa Yuca* were able to borrow money. We stopped at the Seven Eleven and Poncho went to pay for five dollars of gas. Again we would travel without a hot coffee and donut or having enough to buy a beer for the pain at the end of the day. Poncho finished gassing up the car and we got on Highway 111 to begin our trip. It was routine, we had been doing this for almost two weeks. We were all silent, each with our thoughts. We still had two more days before payday and it was becoming a difficult struggle to borrow from friends and family. Everybody was broke. We had a bad harvest and the summer had been cruel. In two days we would be relieved by a good check. But those few days seemed endless. The pain in my leg was a continuous torture. My concern went from being broke to being crippled. I knew several people who had the same conditions and stayed crippled forever. Most injured workers did not have the will to confront the insurance companies. They were ignored and left defenseless to face a miserable future. The idea was terrifying since I depended on my physical abilities to support my family. I was determined to fight in anyway possible to get what I deserved. I had given so much to the industry and the least they could do was to give me proper medical attention.

---

[7] Only five damn dollars

I worked with intense pain all day long. It was obvious my injury was serious and all I was doing was prolonging my situation and increasing my injury. At the end of the day I talked to the Forman about my condition and asked him for the forms to submit a worker's compensation claim. The man hesitated but eventually gave me the forms.

"*Espero que no te estés haciendo péndejo*[8]," he repeated. I never took any crap from anyone, but at that moment I did not need an additional problem, so I stayed calm. We had an argument about the possibilities of my leg being injured somewhere else and that my intent was to blame it on the company to get its insurance. After many threats and warnings, the Forman finally gave me the forms and directions to see the insurance's clinic for the initial analysis of my injury. I could not see a doctor of my choice until one month after the injury; it worried me. I had heard stories of how these clinics would give limited services and sided with the insurance to send workers back to work despite their injuries. Without medical and economic assistance the choices were limited. Many returned to work only to aggravate their condition and remained crippled for the rest of their lives.

The first days were hell. Everything went wrong. It affected my social and emotional life as well as my ability to meet my economic needs. And the pain; it increased as the days went by. My family had plans to attend my sister's graduation. Maria Luisa was graduating from the university in Guadalajara. She was the first to get an education in my family and my mother encouraged everyone to save money to make the trip. My wife and children were thrilled we were going. They loved to go to Guadalajara. It had been quite a while since we took any vacations. But now, with a painful injury and a fruitless harvest season, the possibilities of going were almost gone. I had a

---

[8] I hope you are not faking the injury

car that I wanted to sell to use the money for the trip. I encouraged my wife to go with the kids while I stayed home to continue with the doctor's appointments and treatment. I couldn't make the trip even if I had the means. Just the idea of riding a train for 42 hours terrified me. I could not stay in one position for a prolonged period of time. If I did the pain increased. I knew I would not be able to stand it. The suffering was not worth the thought. Besides, I had to stay. The insurance continued to put doubts on my injury, which was corroborated by the doctor's reports. According to him I was ready to go back to work. In reality my injury was worse. I had lost significant control of my foot and could not feel anything below the knee. My leg was going numb. The pain never went away, day and night. It hurt deep inside my body and my soul. It hurt laying, sitting or standing; the pain was reflected in my expressions. I was not receiving any medicine to alleviate my pain and the only therapy was to submerge my leg in hot water. Therapy was mandatory and I had to drive 30 miles round trip without assistance. I pleaded with workman's compensation about my health and my economic situation. They said they were going by the reports of the doctor who obviously diminished the seriousness of my injury, preventing actions in my favor. I knew it would happen. The doctor and insurance were delaying the medical and financial services to force me to return to work despite the seriousness of my injury. It made me angry. The pain and the worries caused me tremendous stress and frequent emotional outbursts. I always had a bad temper. My children would rather avoid me. My wife patiently tried to console me. She massaged my leg and caressed my hair as she lovingly talked me into believing in possible solutions. She wanted to cancel the trip to Guadalajara.

"If you don't go we won't go. We cannot leave you here alone while you are sick," she argued.

"*Es un infierno aquí conmigo así como estoy de furioso⁹*," I said as I encouraged her to go.

I felt tears rolling down my face as I waved my family good-bye. They were going to Guadalajara by train with my mother and other members of my family. I was sad to see them go and I knew María Elena felt the same. My wife hesitated to leave me behind and pleaded to the last minute for me to accompany them. But she agreed that it was the best for all. They would have a few peaceful days while I continued with the procedures mandated by work man's compensation. We all hoped our situation had improved by the time they returned home. I limped to the car to make the trip back across the border to Calexico.

I walked in circles inside my empty house for a while; then I sat on the couch. I felt sad, tired, and lonely. It was the beginning of a long, painful wait for my injury to heal. I hoped the solitude would help me find composure. I needed to take things calmly and make the right decisions. For now, all I could do was wait. I went to one of the children's bedroom and pulled a mattress to the living room right in front of the television. I went to the bedroom and from under the bed pulled out a bottle of brandy. "*Presidente¹⁰*" read the label. I wondered if "*el Presidente*" could ease my terrible pains. Maybe if I got really drunk the pain would go away and I could sleep and forget my problems for a few hours. I smiled at the thought and took the first shot. I frown at the impact of the strong burning liquor going down my throat. I quenched my mouth, sucking on a lemon with salt, hoping the juice would ease the strong taste. By the third shot my mouth and throat got use to the burning sensation of "*el Presidente.*" The pain began to ease as I got intoxicated. I tried to watch television but could not concentrate on the programs. My mind kept

---

⁹ It is hell near me as enraged as I am.

¹⁰ President – Mexican brandy brand name.

wandering away. I could not get the unnerving events out of my mind: my dismay at how I was treated by the doctor and insurance continued. I could not believe it. After all the years of working for this industry and this is the way they paid me back. I let out an angry scream that echoed through the empty house. I had given them my best years, all my youth working in the fields and now I was crippled and unable to work. All I had left was the pain of my useless leg. The hurt was gone for now because of the strong liquor, but it was sure to return after the effects were gone. I kept repeating to myself "Why did it happen to me? Why!" I screamed, sobbing, letting out my rage. I laid on the mattress thinking. Memories of my childhood passed through my mind like a motion picture. The images when I first came to California were clear. I remembered clearly how happy we were the first time we crossed the border with dreams of a good future; dreams that now had turned into a terrible nightmare.

IT WAS THE FIRST TIME

It was the first time I ever crossed the line. I had heard about it many times from my father who crossed *La línea*[11] almost daily to work the fields. He said everyone spoke English, a very strange language I heard only from people who had learned a few words and phrases, like my father who enjoyed speaking to us, bragging how good he could speak, almost like the Gringos. I also heard about it from some children from the neighborhood who would bring out their toys purchased *en el otro lado*[12]. They said that their parents usually brought them wonderful toys and delicious treats that could not be found on this side of the border. I had dreams about crossing it, but I could not picture how it would be. In my mind it was like a magic land with all kinds of fantastic things to play with or to eat. I imagined beautiful gardens full of flowers with games for the children and places for people to rest. I could not wait until the day I could cross it. I knew it would be soon because I heard the conversations about getting our papers, our own *micas*[13] soon.

It was early in the morning when we came to the border crossing of

---

[11] The border

[12] On the other side

[13] Immigration cards

11

Calexico, California. We were all very nervous, except my father who was familiar with the process of presenting his documents and being questioned by tall white men speaking English.

"Where are your documents?" The man would say mixed with a very funny Spanish; "*¿Donde estar sus documentos*[14]?"

I could not understand either one. I almost broke out in laughter when I heard them, but I stopped, thinking they might get mad and not allow me to cross. Finally we were allowed to pass the immigration check point. We walked in, crossed First Street and continued to Second Street, the downtown area where all the businesses are. Right away I saw differences; the streets were all paved and very clean. The stores were similar to the ones on the other side but with a better appearance. The most noticeable difference was the things inside the stores. There were toys and things to eat; some of them were strange, but had a delicious smell. My father said we would eat hamburgers and hot dogs later after we took our things to our new apartment.

"What are hamburgers and hot dogs?" I asked.

"You will see later," answered my father.

We walked for many blocks to get to our new apartment. As we walked we saw the houses, old but well kept and all the yards had fences, grass and trees. In my old neighborhood in Mexicali, the houses were old and rundown; some were made out of scrap wood or adobe, some had dirt or cement floors and the yards were barren. There were no sidewalks or pavement and the streets were full of holes. It was so bad that people had difficulty driving their cars on them. After walking for a while we came to a park. There were many games for children: swings, slides and the most exciting of all, a merry-go-round. This was the first time I had seen one. Our apartment was right across the street

---

[14] Where are your documents?

from the park. My sister Silvia, age seven, and I, age nine, were very excited. We were actually going to live across the street from a park with many things to play on and have fun. We had never experienced such excitement before. Even my brother Rafael who was only three years old was excited. Our apartment was very small; one bedroom and a small kitchen/dinning room combination. Silvia, Rafael, and I slept on the floor over some blankets while my parents and younger sister Maria Luisa, only eight months old, slept on the only bed the apartment had. Even though we lived in very crowded quarters, we were happy because it was much better than what we had back in our old neighborhood, or at least it seemed that way. The most exciting thing, for now, was that we lived across the street from the park with trees to climb and games to play with.

Our first visit to the park was a life experience, hard to forget. When we arrived we saw some children. They spoke English and we could not understand, a very strange feeling that I felt many times during the first months of living across the border. My sister and I looked at each other not knowing what to do and we tried to interact, but we were rejected so we decided to play on our own. That day we played on the swings and slides and later we sat down to watch how other children played with the merry-go-round. We waited until the other children left so we could try riding it. I pushed the large wheel the same way I saw the other children do it. When it was going fast I would jump on it to ride with my sister who waited clinched to a handle with a frightened look, scared of falling off. The merry-go-round could spin very fast and it was tilted, giving the riders a sensation of going up and down as it turned. I was almost thrown off when I pushed it as fast as I could and then jumped on it. After a while I got to master the process and I made it go faster and faster. It was great going to the park; it was the first time we ever had so much fun since we never had access to such exciting games. In my old neighborhood we had other means of playing. Our street had been under renovation for many months. There was a huge trench for new drains that ran from one side to the other. The trench did not allow cars to transit so the children could play on the mounds formed by trench's dirt. We played trench war, throwing mud balls at each other. The other popular activity for boys in my neighborhood was boxing. There were several professional boxers living nearby and during the afternoons we would see their training sessions. We were encouraged to learn to punch. It was common to have tournaments where we had matches between boys of the same age and size.

I missed my friends, and here in my new home I had none. I did not have the means to communicate with other children and my sister and I wondered if we would ever make friends. We just had to learn how to speak that strange language.

The language barrier became a bigger problem when we went to school. The first day was nerve wracking. We were intimidated and frustrated to listen to all these people speak and not being able to understand what they said. It felt like I was living on another planet. We were somewhat shy and hesitated to approach other children. No one spoke Spanish; it was not allowed, and not knowing anyone made it more difficult to get acquainted. It is difficult to be the new kid in school and to make friends without knowing how to speak the language. It is something that I really hated the first months of living in California. My parents, being seasonal farm workers moved very often following the crops. Sometimes they moved up to six different times in one year. There were times when my sister and I were just beginning to find friends when we had to move once again and once again we were the new kids in a strange school.

My sister and I tried very hard to learn English. We were fortunate that we were sent to an early morning class. It started at 7:00 AM and lasted one hour daily. The class was conducted by a teacher named Mr. Lopez, who was very friendly and always encouraged us to learn the language, he taught us some very efficient techniques.

I remember him saying, "The more you practice your vocabulary the faster you will learn to speak. Add five words, daily, that you need in your activities, and use them as much as possible. Daily! Master them to increase your ability to speak fluently."

My sister and I took it very seriously. We spoke the words we learned daily and kept a log of them. We reviewed them over and over and pretended that we were American and had conversations in English. We had fun with it; we used the words we knew and combined them with words we invented when we spoke in the presence of the people in our old neighborhood. "Hey! Hello my friend, wishi washu washa?" Meaning, according to us, "Hello, my friend, do you want to play?" Our friends and relatives were impressed and complimented our parents for our fast English acquisition, not knowing that we were inventing most of the words. My sister and I had many laughs; we planned the meaning of our invented vocabulary and practiced it in our conversations at home.

Our first days in school were very intimidating but interesting. We felt like being in another world. The classrooms were so different from the ones in my old school. They had doors with ornaments and the room was surrounded with colorful words I did not understand. I could try to read them but they made no sense to me. Our class in Mexicali had no doors or windows. We were lucky we had a roof and a floor made of cement. I remember having to bring a broom from my house to sweep it. Each child was assigned one day of the month to sweep and throw the trash out. We were rotated taking turns to cover the entire school year. The classroom walls in my new school were painted and the floor had tile. The students' work was displayed on the walls on bulletin boards that had drawings and pictures. And also, all those words…. Words I did not understand. The teacher, Miss Charles, had a desk where she had pictures of her family and ornaments and cacti. She liked miniature cactus plants. She actually had a collection of miniature pots with all kinds of small cacti. The cacti were near a sink where students could wash their hands.

When I first came in the classroom, the students looked at me with curiosity and murmured to each other. I knew they were talking about me, but I could not understand. If I could only know what they were saying; it really kept me wondering. It seemed like the teacher introduced me to all the third grade class. Some of the girls wiggled and looked at each other whispering God knows what. Miss Charles was very pleasant; but firm, her class was always quiet and working. The students liked her and respected her. Her activities were very interesting even for me who did not understand what she said. I could relate to the lesson by the visuals she used. My favorite subject was math; I was the best at multiplying and dividing and best of all I did not need to speak English to understand numbers. Speaking Spanish was not allowed in the class but during recess I managed to find out how to say the essentials. Asking permission to go to the bathroom was the first most important phrase my sister and I learned the first day of school. In time, we learned many words and Mr. Lopez, our English teacher, encouraged us. He was always very nice and friendly with all the newcomers. Mr. Lopez knew how to encourage students to learn the language fast. I collected words daily like he said, and practiced daily. I found out their meaning and was always looking for someone to say them to. At first it was just my sister, but later, as I made friends, I could practice more. Soon my sister and I were speaking phrases to our parents. Some were real, but others, the ones my sister and I made up, we used only to impress our parents and friends who did not speak the language. We tried not to play our English Language Development Game with our English speaking friends; they would probably have made fun of us. A few weeks after we crossed the border and went to Rockwood, our first school, it was time to move on after the seasonal crops. We were just getting used to the school routine, making friends and communicating in as many ways as possible. It was a strange sensation to know that once again it was time to move to a strange, uncertain place. I felt emptiness in my stomach and many thoughts crossed my mind about the loneliness, the struggle of adapting to uncertain place and people. What could be waiting for us? We heard our parents, talking excitedly about it. They said it was going to be good for us, that there was work harvesting lettuce and we would have lots of money. My parents had never done this kind of work but a friend of my father invited us to come to Salinas, California, and he would show us around and help us establish ourselves and find work. It was a very sad to move; we had just made friends, we complained, and were doing well in school, we argued, and we were learning the language, we pleaded. But my father did not want to hear about it and my mom calmly agreed that it would be good for us.

MY FIRST MIGRATION

It was very early in the morning; the sun was not out yet. We had packed all of our belongings in three large pieces of luggage and a cardboard box. We did not have much; our clothes, a few cooking utensils, an alarm clock and a radio. Don Juanito, my father's friend, and his daughter Ana came to pick us up in their car. It was a large, four-door Ford in rather good shape.

"I just tuned up my car," he bragged. "Salinas is far, about 550 miles, but the car is in good condition and we will get there. It will be a long trip and we have to cross Los Angeles. We must get going fast and avoid all the traffic or we will be delayed even more."

"What traffic?" I asked Don Juanito.

"Ooohhhhh, you will see!" he laughed. "You have never seen so many cars together in your life," he replied.

We loaded part of our things in the trunk of the car with the other luggage. One of the pieces of luggage was too big, so we put it in the bottom area of the back seat where I was sitting, and my mother said it would be a good place because I was so small. I could sit and put my feet on the luggage.

"It will be uncomfortable, but you are a strong boy," she said encouragingly with her smile.

She knew I would not complain.

We were very crowded in the car with four adults and four children. My sister rode in front with Don Juanito and Ana. In the back seat, my mother and father each sat carrying one of the smaller children, and of course there was me with my feet on the large piece of luggage.

We started on our long journey to Salinas. At first we could not see anything, as it was very dark, so the children went to sleep. I kept my eyes open; I loved to look out the window for interesting landmarks or buildings or anything that was on the way. I remember our trip from Guadalajara to Mexicali a few years ago. We rode the train for three days and nights; it was such a long trip compared to this one. This trip was shorter and more exciting. I kept thinking of all the things I would see along the freeway. I was anxious to see the heavy traffic in Los Angeles and the 101 freeway.

"*El Camino Real*[15]," Don Juanito said, referring to the freeway.

My father and him kept talking about it most of the way. They talked about how it was first made as a trail for the missionaries to travel from San Diego all the way to San Francisco, with many missions along the way to rest. Many of the missions still existed and we would see some of them along the road.

The first one hundred miles we traveled on a two lane highway. Later we merged into a very big highway, Interstate 10,

"*El Dies*[16]," said Anita.

She asked Don Juanito to stop for a restroom break in one of the gas stations that had a hamburger stand. We all got out and stretched. My mother and father went to buy something to eat.

"What do you want?" she asked us.

---

[15] The Royal Road

[16] The ten freeway

I asked for a hamburger and fries while others had hotdogs. We rested for a short time and went to the restroom. After we ate it was time to go once more. We would not stop again until we had crossed Los Angeles and the heavy traffic. *"El Dies"* was very interesting; first there were some cars but as we got near Los Angeles the number of cars increased rapidly. Soon the three lanes were all full of cars, which were going very fast. We were on the right side of the freeway where the slower cars traveled.

"We want to be safe," said Ana.

She did not like her father to drive fast like the others. I sadly saw all the cars passing us. I did not like it; I wished Don Juanito would go faster than the others and not allow anyone to pass us. I wanted us to be number one, faster than the rest. I counted all the cars we passed; most of them were large trucks, mobile homes, run down cars or some cars with *viejitos*[17] who were more cautious than Don Juanito. Many of the faster cars were so beautiful, new and modern.

"They belong to rich people," Ana said.

There were many movie stars living nearby in Hollywood where they made movies. We were all amazed thinking that perhaps some of the drivers of the beautiful cars were celebrities.

"If we were to cross Los Angeles at a later time there would be more, many, many, many more cars than now," Don Juanito was telling us. "It would be so crowded that we would have to go very slow and sometimes even stop and wait." He bragged about how he was saving time by coming so early; he was very proud of his smart decision.

Los Angeles was huge, a sea of cars traveling on large highways surrounded by many bridges and buildings. I had never imagined a place like this in my whole life. Our eyes turned to one side then to the other,

---

[17] Old people

excited, trying to catch a glimpse of everything around us. There were so many beautiful buildings, some very tall, the tallest we had ever seen. It was so different than our old neighborhood in Mexicali. I wondered if we would someday live in a beautiful house like the ones we saw along the way.

"There is the junction to 101," my father said.

We passed a sign that announced that the freeway was near. We got onto Freeway 101 and later the number of cars diminished as we moved away from the largest city we had seen in our lives. For an hour all we talked about was all the new things we saw. We felt so lucky to have seen them all. I asked my father and mother if we would be able to earn money to buy one of those new cars by working in the lettuce fields. My father said that we would try to buy a car, but it would be a used *camioneta*[18] to fit all our things and all the kids when we moved after the crops.

"The new cars are only for rich people. We are only farm workers," said my father like it was our destiny.

I wished we could someday, maybe, just maybe, have a new car, but deep inside, I knew it was just a dream, a wish not too easy to get. My mother said we should be happy; we were very lucky just to be in California and to have work and a roof for shelter. We knew many people that were worse off than us back in our *barrio*[19].

The farm workers' camp was not very big; it had six long barracks to house 40 single male workers each, two other large structures for the toilets and showers and a large dining room and kitchen where food for all the workers was prepared. In addition, across a large yard, there were three small houses for families. All the buildings formed a perimeter around a big yard where people parked their cars or played games to

---

[18] Station Wagon

[19] Neighborhood

entertain themselves after work. The camp was completely surrounded by large fields of lettuce. We were greeted by "*el Campero*[20]." He greeted "Don Juanito," who in turn introduced my father and the rest of the family. Standing by the house was a very short lady and a tall boy looking on smiling, trying to listen to the conversation. *El Campero* was explaining that our house was not ready, that it would take about a week before we could live in it. He said that in the meantime we could use one of the large barracks for *las cuadrillas de lechugueros*[21]," since they would not arrive until a few weeks later when the harvest season began. *Los lechugueros* harvested the lettuce when it was fully grown. For now the lettuce was small and my parents would work in a *cuadrilla del cortito*[22] who thinned and weeded the lettuce fields. *El Cortito*[23] was used to shave the excess plants off the beds of lettuce, leaving only one every ten inches, the space needed by the lettuce to grow properly. It was a grueling job; the hoe was so short that people had to bend over and swing their arm repeatedly and swiftly to cut off excess plants and weeds.

El Campero took my father to a shed where he could chose some beds and mattresses; he told my father that for the mean time we would have to buy a small electric stove to cook since the barracks did not have a kitchen. The men took the beds, a table, and some chairs to the barrack. My mother, my sister, and I helped to arrange the furniture. The barrack was very big; on one side my mother put two beds together to form a large bed for my father, mother, and Maria Luisa. On the other side Rafael, Silvia and I each had a bed. My mother put all the cooking utensils on a table in the middle of the room; she left a space for the stove

---

[20] Camp caretaker

[21] Lettuce harvesters crew

[22] Short hoe crew

[23] Short hoe

we would buy the next day and talked about getting an additional table for us to eat on. The way my mother arranged the furniture made the impression that the large barrack was a three room house.

My mother woke us up early in the morning: "Hurry," she said, "we are going with Ana and Don Juanito to the flea market to buy the things we need."

As we dressed, she kept telling us what Delfina, el *Campero's* wife, had told her about *"la pulga*[24]." Delfina said there are so many things to see and that we could find what we needed at very reasonable prices. Some of the things were new but most were used.

"If we are lucky we could find great bargains! We only need a stove, but if we see something that we can use we will get it," my father said excitedly about the visit to the flea market.

We did not have a lot of money but there were some things we could not do without and we were forced to buy them.

"*Que neblina tan fea*[25]," my mother said, as she insisted that we cover our heads.

Everyone said the fog was bad for your health. *La brisa* made it very cold outside and we didn't want anyone to get sick. We hurried to the car and got in quickly.

"Do you think we escaped safely from *la brisa?*" we asked mother,

"Yes for now," she said, "but you have to be careful always because here we will have lots of it every day."

The fog in Salinas is always very dense because it is near the ocean. On many days the sun will not be seen until late in the day.

"*La Pulga* is on the parking lot of a drive-in," said Ana.

"A what?" we asked her.

---

[24] Flea market

[25] What bad fog

"A drive-in, It is a theater that you drive into to see a movie from your car," said Ana.

"See a movie from a car?" we asked, puzzled by the unknown.

Ana nodded, "They have speakers and you put them on your window for you to hear," she explained.

"What happens if you do not have a car?" I asked.

"They will not let you in," said Ana, "but don't worry. I will invite you when we come," she said laughing.

We all encouraged our father to hurry and get enough money to buy a car; we all wanted to be able to go.

"Some day," said my mother. "We will see when we start working."

There were so many booths with all kinds of things. Everything you can imagine you could find it in *La pulga*. There were clothes, cooking utensils, furniture, appliances, televisions, radios, record players, and many toys. Most were used; some were in good condition, others were not. There were some booths where they sold food. They had *menudo*, *tacos, tortas* [26] and sodas where we had something to eat. We saw many Americans selling but the majority that went to buy were Mexican farm workers. They all went to get the bargains and buy essential items to get through the season. Don Juanito said that it was best to buy the used items; they were cheap and people did not know if they could take them when they followed the crop to another faraway place. There was only so much you could pack in their car. It was not worth buying new and expensive things if there was the possibility of giving them away or be disposed in the trash.

My father found a used electric stove. It seemed to be in good condition.

The American man said, "*Es muy bueno. Muy barato. Cómpralo,*

---

[26] Tripe stew, light snack bight, Mexican sandwich.

ándale[27]. It is only twenty dollars."

My mother began to bargain; she was very good at it as bargaining was very common in Mexico. She used to tell us, "*la gente pobre tiene que regatear pa' hacerla[28]*".

My father ended up paying only 12 dollars, and he said we could use what we had saved to buy other things. My brother and sister wanted some toys, but we all wanted a television most.

"No," said my father, "not until we establish ourselves. Then we will buy all the things you want."

La Pulga was fun; we got the things we needed and my mother bought a small tricycle and a ball for us to play with. I was too old for a tricycle but I could help the younger ones to use it. I was used to playing with them; sometimes they were all I had to play with and we all tried to make the best of it.

"You are the oldest," my mother said, "and you need to help out with your smaller brothers and sisters."

It was very early when my mother woke me up; we had to get ready to register at our new school. She hurried us to dress and get towels to cover our heads. We had to walk 50 meters to the common showers since our barrack did not have these services. My sister started sobbing and complaining. She was afraid to take a shower in this huge room full of open showers. She was always concerned someone would come in and see her naked.

"*Me van a ver[29]*," she would say, sobbing.

As we walked out we covered our heads because of the fog; it was so dense it felt like it was raining. We walked towards a light across the yard from us. That was all we could see through the dense fog. My mother

---

[27] It is good, inexpensive, buy it; come on.

[28] Poor people have to bargain to make ends meet.

[29] They are going to see me.

made sure there was no one inside the showers. She then went inside each, the men's and the women's showers, and opened the water for my sister and me. She made sure the water temperature was appropriate and told us to scrub hard behind the ears as she stood guard at the entrance of the buildings. We dried ourselves in a hurry; it was very cold and we were not used to it. We dressed, covered our heads, and headed back to our barrack.

My mother made breakfast for us as she was telling us how Delfina had offered to give us a ride to school; it was too far from the camp to walk. We would be able to ride the bus the next day together with her son Fernando.

"The important thing is to get them registered," Delfina said.

We got in the car and were greeted by Fernando.

"Good morning!" he said, in English.

We answered in Spanish, *"Buenos Días!"*

He asked our names in English and we both answered in Spanish. I felt uncomfortable speaking to a stranger in the little English I knew. I was nervous and could see that my sister was, too. We had to drive to the main street through a short dirt road that outlined one of the lettuce fields. At the corner was a hamburger stand that had a giant white rooster on top.

"¡Mira mamá un gallo enorme[30]!" I asked Fernando, *"¿Qué es[31]?"*

"It is the Dairy Queen. They sell hamburgers, sodas and ice cream. I like the chocolate dipped better than anything else," he answered.

My sister and I looked at Fernando puzzled; we had not understood what he had said. We knew some words and phrases but not enough to understand. I asked if he could tell us in Spanish.

---

[30] Look mother an enormous rooster.

[31] What is it?

"You don't speak English?" he asked.

Now he was puzzled. He tried to explain but had some difficulty.

"He is not very fluent in Spanish," Delfina explained. "The only reason he speaks a little is because I don't speak English very well and I insist that he learn to speak the two languages. He is not around me all the time so he does not practice enough."

"It will be good for you," my mother pointed out. "You can help Fernando practice some Spanish and you can learn English from him."

It was very unfortunate that Fernando was not in a classroom with us. We all were in different grades. It would have been a great way to adapt to this school.

My mother had to complete registration forms and show proof of immunization. The secretary also asked for documents of residence and my mother proudly pulled them out and presented them.

"*Nada mas tenemos unos meses aquí, están nuevesitas*[32]," my mother tried to explain.

The lady looked at my mother and smiled as she thanked her. My mother was so excited that we were accepted, but then became concerned when she was told we could stay and return on the bus. It would be the first time we would ride on a bus to school. Delfina reassured my mother that all would be fine. Fernando would help us get around and return home.

"They will learn fast and do it on their own soon, just like all the other students," Delfina said.

My mother gave us each thirty-five cents to pay for lunch.

"Don't lose the money; if you do they will not give you your lunch," my mother said as she saw us go to our classroom.

Santa Rita School was more intimidating than Rockwood. The

---

[32] We have only been here for a few months, they are new.

teacher was friendly but did not have full control of the class and she would lose her temper. Sometimes I was glad I did not understand what she said when some students made her mad. During the first part of the class we did writing and reading. I liked reading; I could read many words because of my skills in Spanish but I still did not understand most of them. I missed Mr. Lopez from Rockwood; here they did not have anyone to help us learn English and for some reason I could not understand. I was not able to communicate as I was doing just a few days before at Rockwood. I felt dumb. Later in the day we did math; I was happy when we came to that subject because I could prove I was a good student. I was very good in multiplication and division and the skills I had learned in Mexicali seemed to be more advanced than those of the children in my class. We did a multiplication tables drill where I received first place. My teacher was very impressed and smiled as she patted me on the shoulder, showing her approval. Now I wished I knew what she said, but even if I did not understand, I felt a great sensation of acceptance. I heard her say my name, among other words, to the rest of the class. She smiled, I smiled, some of the students smiled, but there were some that made a terrible frown. Like everywhere I experienced, there is always a bully or two who make the life of the new student miserable, and I was the new student. *¡O Dios*[33]*!* Somehow I felt things would not go well during recess.

The bell rang for lunch and the class formed a line and walked to the cafeteria. At the door there was lady next to cash register collecting money from the students. I put my hand in my pocket to get my money and found only the quarter. I looked for the dime but could not find it. I was concerned; I was not going to get my lunch. As I stood in line wondering what to do, I saw how the lady sent some students to an office just to the side of the cafeteria. I watched carefully and figured out that

[33] Ohh God!

they must have problems with their money just like me. As I got closer I tried to listen to what they were saying. In front of me was one of the class bullies who did not have enough money either.

"Go to that office and ask them to lend you a quarter and then come back," the lady told the bully.

As I came to the lady I showed her my quarter, I inhaled deeply and said "No have dime."

She smiled and said, "Ohh! You lost your dime." She pointed at the door and said, "Go there."

I felt relieved; I was going to eat lunch after all. As I walked inside the office and formed at the end of a small line, I continued to listen, I wanted to figure out what to say. In front of me was the bully. He turned to me and said something I did not understand. His tone of voice and his expression meant it was not something nice. I just smiled. He was next, so he turned around to a lady who was taking names and lending money to the students.

"I lost a quarter," the bully said.

I listened carefully thinking about what to say based on what the bully said. My turn came. I was nervous.

"I am a dime," I said.

With dismay, I heard strong laughter from the other students; apparently making fun of what I had just said. I felt the earth go down beneath my feet. I was so embarrassed. Worst of all, out of the corner of my eye, I saw the bully laughing and repeating what I had said and encouraging the other students to make fun of me. The lady snapped at the students, ushering them out.

"It's OK!" she said smiling.

She handed me the dime and pointed to the cafeteria. I went in the cafeteria following the line to pick my tray of food. I wanted to make myself invisible so no one could see me, especially the students who heard what I had said. How stupid of me! I could have said, "Me want one dime," but now it was too late. I looked for Fernando; my sister had come to lunch earlier with the younger students. I saw Fernando waving at me; I walked through the isles to get there faster when I heard a whistle. Cutting was not allowed, and I needed to sit with my group. The whistle got the attention of many students. I felt everyone was looking at me, teasing me about what I said. I felt their eyes, how they followed me, and watched me as I ate as fast as I could.

When my table was dismissed, we walked out of the cafeteria in line to go out in the playground. Outside I found Fernando who was waiting for me.

"*¿Qué te paso*[34]?" he asked smiling.

He had heard about the dime incident. I frowned and said to myself, "*Que burrada, Seré el hazme reír de todos*", *mejor ya no voy a hablar*[35]." We walked away to the swings. Fernando kept telling me that it was OK, but he teased me saying that they would laugh at me for a week or so. I kept thinking about it all day. If I talk they will laugh at me; if I don't, I will not learn.

I tried to avoid the bully but it was not possible. He always found a way to tease me. I was not afraid of him; I was more concerned about getting into trouble. My mother would be very worried and that was the last thing I wanted. I knew I could fight with him and win; I had to fight other boy *en mi Barrio*[36]. I had been in boxing tournaments, participating and winning several times. I had also played on a soccer team. I was short but very tough. But once when I got in a fight in school, in self-defense, they suspended me and my mother was very worried.

---

[34] What happened to you?

[35] How dumb, I will be the laughing stock of all, I rather not speak anymore.

[36] In my neighborhood

"*Pórtate bien*[37]," she would say.

My mother wanted me to go to school, so I always tried my best to stay out of trouble.

Later in the afternoon the class lined up and a girl and I were assigned to get two balls to play with. They looked like soccer balls, about the same size but smoother. The class was Physical Education and the teacher said we would play kick ball. "*¿Patear la pelota*[38]?" I wondered how the game was played. We came to a small baseball field. I had played baseball *en mi Barrio,* but this seemed to be different. Students lined up in the field like playing baseball but instead of bats we were kicking a large ball. We would catch it with our hands and try to throw the kickers out. I laughed to myself, thinking, "*Qué mensos*[39]," "what a stupid game; why don't we just play baseball?"

Most of the students missed the ball so badly they looked funny. I had difficulty staying calm and not laughing out loud. One of the bullies even fell down when he kicked the ground. Everyone rolled their eyes and teased him until the teacher put a stop to it. The ones, who did connect the ball, kicked it very weakly or in the wrong direction. Then it was my turn. I was caught off guard when the teacher called me. I started to the plate hesitating; I wanted to be sure it was my turn. One student, acting like a pitcher, rolled the ball to me and I kicked it very hard. Everyone started cheering when they saw the ball fly to the outfield.

"Home run!" they shouted. "Run, run!" Wow!

They were all excited. As I ran around the bases several kids went running after the ball far into the field. Now I did not think the game was stupid. It had made me very popular in my class. It seemed that I was on my way to getting some friends.

---

[37] Behave

[38] Kick ball

[39] How dumb

At the end of the day, I walked towards the pick up area to look for my sister and Fernando. I saw Fernando waving and to his side my sister carrying her work. He called me to hurry; he wanted to get a good seat on the bus. On the way home we shared our experiences. We joked a little about the "dime incident." We were the last to get off the bus. The bus dropped us at the corner where the Dairy Queen was. We talked about how wonderful it would be to taste one of those chocolate dipped ice creams.

"There are three sizes: small, medium and large, and they cost five, ten and fifteen cents. The large ones have two scoops of vanilla ice cream and the chocolate covers them all. I like the small one best. It's the perfect size. Besides, it's easy to buy it. I is easier to get a nickel than fifteen cents," said Fernando. We all laughed, agreeing about the cost of the ice cream and starting the long walk to the camp.

My mother was waiting for us at the door; she let go a sigh of relief when she saw us.

"*Que bueno que llegaron. Estaba preocupada*[40]," she said.

She was worried but she calmed down when she saw how excited we were. We told her all that had happened as she served diner.

"Your father will be here soon. He said he would get an advance from today's work and take us to try the hamburgers and ice cream *en el gallo*[41]," she told us excitedly knowing we would like the surprise.

Later that day we walked to the Dairy Queen. We could see the big white rooster with a green crest from far away. It got bigger and bigger as we came closer. We could smell the hamburgers and fries before we got there. But the thing that was on my mind was the wonderful ice cream. I was wondering if it was as delicious as it looked.

One week later, we moved to the family house. It was not very big

---

[40] I am glad you came, I was worried.

[41] At the rooster

33

but it had all the services inside. There were two rooms: the bedroom and a combination kitchen, dining room and living room. The kitchen had a gas stove; there was no need for the electric stove we had purchased a few days before.

"We will save it for the future," said my mother; anticipating we would move again soon.

The best thing was the inside bathroom. It was private, just for us. No one will see me naked again and I will not freeze when I take a shower anymore, I thought. The following Sunday, my mother woke us up early.

"*Vamos a la pulga. Apúrense*[42]," she said.

We were going to the flea market again and she was rushing us. My mother had started working and now the family was getting two checks. We had a better house and my mother thought it would be a good idea to get a television.

"Maybe we can find one at the flea market," my mother said.

She was excited that we would get our first television. We had seen some the last time we went. *La pulga* was crowded; many farm workers went as a pastime activity. There was not much to do for them in Salinas or the nearby towns. There was only one radio station that played Mexican music and only for two hours in the afternoon. The theater showed Mexican movies only on Wednesday afternoon and Saturdays. The movies were really old: *Piporro, Pedro Infante y Luís Aguilar*[43]. Sometimes they showed movies de *El Santo*[44]. I always begged to go; he was our favorite wrestler and movie star. He would fight all kinds of monsters and bad men. The audience, all farm workers, cheered in excitement, forgetting their problems and pains, as *El Santo* defeated the criminals.

---

[42] We are going to the flea market, hurry.

[43] Popular Mexican singers and actors.

[44] The Saint

My mother found a small black and white television.

"The television is small. It will not take to much room in the car when we move," she said. "This is good for now."

My mother bargained a good price. Only thirty dollars and we were allowed to test the television before we bought it. The television worked well. It had a small problem; sometimes we had held the channel dial in place using a folded paper, to get a clear picture. It really didn't matter since we could only get one channel. Once we set the dial, we did not have to move it again. The only programs we liked to watch were cartoons and they were shown only on Saturday mornings. It was our first television ever and we were very happy to have it, even if we did not understand what was said in most of the programs.

We could hardly wait for Saturday. We wished time would fly so we could see cartoons on our very own television. In school everything was going fine; the bullies had left me alone and some even spoke to me and allowed me to play other popular games during recess. I learned to play Four Square and Tetherball. I always tried to be the best in all. We continued to improve our English and could communicate more with students and staff. We were also able to make new friends. I was always puzzled when I saw students who I knew were Mexican refuse to speak to us in Spanish or make believe they did not understand us. Some spoke it a little but talked weird.

"No comprender[45]," they would say "No hablando Español[46]."

I told my mother and father and they joked that I would be the same when I learned to speak properly.

"When we go to Guadalajara you can do the same. You can tell all your friends and cousins "No entender que decir[47]," my father said teasing

---

[45] I don't understand

[46] I don't speak Spanish

[47] I don't understand what you say

us.

We all laughed, but I knew I would never be like that. Maybe the students were just following the rules; it was prohibited to speak Spanish and perhaps they were afraid to get in trouble.

Saturday came and I was awakened by the smell of food. My mother was making lunch for herself and my father and breakfast for us. I woke up early every day; I loved to eat tacos and hot oatmeal. After eating I would lie on my bed until the time the cartoons started, and then I would wake Sylvia and Rafael. Maria Luisa was taken to the babysitter when my parents left. The babysitter would check on us during the day. Cartoons and children's programs started at six in the morning and ended at ten. After that there were other programs we did not care to watch. After watching we would go outside and play. Fernando would come and play with us.

"Did you see the bus of people that went by the camp this morning?" he asked.

"No, why?" we asked Fernando trying to get more information from him.

"I think that *la cuadrilla del cortito* is working next to the camp," said Fernando. "You want to go and watch?"

"Yea!" we answered. "It will be exciting to see."

We walked towards the fields around the camp. Far away we saw a large group of people. They were all bent over striking the soil with a short hoe. They were thinning lettuce; a process where workers cut off excess plants. They leave one plant every ten inches providing the proper space for lettuce to develop properly. Once in a while, the *desahijadores*[48] would standup and try to straighten their backs, rest for a few seconds then bend over again. As we got closer we could hear talking. The

---

[48] Thinners

workers would engage in conversations to kill the time and forget about the pain their bodies felt from bending all day long. I heard my name called and I turned. It was my father asking what we were doing there. We asked if we could stay. He asked *el Mayordomo*[49] and he agreed with the condition that we stay off the beds and don't step on the lettuce. I went close to my mother to watch her work. She looked very tired. Pain was reflected in her face as she swung her arm to shave the excess lettuce with the hoe. My mother had not yet learned the basic movements and struggled to keep up with the rest of the workers. She had to keep up or she would not receive pay. In desperation my father would thin the lettuce very fast on his row; he would go ahead of everyone and return on my mother's row; helping her to keep the pace. My mother winced as she tried to straighten up to rest. She struggled to reach the end of her row. As the people finished their rows, they gathered around a water container to drink, and then continued to a new row. Near the bus we saw some extra *cortitos*. I asked the foreman if I could get a hoe to learn to thin and help my mother. The foreman laughed in approval, patted my back, and agreed to let me try. He only asked me to be careful. My father showed me how to thin. He showed me how to swing the hoe, to hit the row deep enough to shave the small lettuce. He also showed me how to walk bending down. To move ahead, I had to step by crossing one leg over the other sideways.

"I want to do it, too," said my sister.

Fernando just watched. I started slowly but learned quickly. Within a few minutes I could thin very slowly but acceptably.

"He is going to be a good worker when he grows up," said the foreman.

I started to help my mother. I would start in front of her so that when she reached the part I thinned she could get up and rest as she

---

[49] The Forman

37

walked in front of me to continue. Between the two of us, my mother went ahead of the crew where she would have more time to rest. She smiled and caressed my hair in appreciation for my help.

"*Lonche! Lonche*[50]!" said the foreman.

It was time to eat. Everyone dropped their hoes and hurried to the bus to rest and have their meals.

"*Vamos a comer*[51]," said my mother as we followed her to the bus.

The people sat in small groups laughing and joking. Lunch was a welcomed and much awaited time to rest. We sat close to other workers, friends of my father.

"Your son is very good. He learns fast; no doubt he will be a good worker soon," said one man.

They laughed and teased each other about how I would be a better worker than they were.

"Well, he is young and has energy, but he will go to school instead," said my mother.

"I can come and work on the weekends," I said, very proud as my mother hugged me.

She was so happy I had come and was able to help. After a while, we started walking home. We did not want Delfina, Maria Luisa's babysitter, to worry; we had not told her where we were going. We were very excited about all the work we had done. I felt proud. I wanted to be the best thinner someday so I could help my mother.

"*¡Los Lechugueros! ¡Los Lechugueros!*" we heard Fernando shouting.

Gasping for air he tried to tell us about the arrival of the lettuce harvesters. A bus was parking in the yard next to the big barracks. Men began downloading their belongings packed in cardboard boxes and bags. Only a few had luggage and they were old and rundown. The men

---

[50] Lunch, lunch

[51] Lets go eat

were teasing each other about being lazy and how they would quit the job in a few days.

Lettuce harvesters had a high social status among farm workers. It was a very demanding job and many people would not dare to try to work. It required skills difficult to acquire and it was extremely exhausting. The crews who thinned or harvested other crops earned their salary by the hour; the lettuce harvesters' salary was by piece worked, meaning that workers would get paid at a rate based on production. The more boxes the crew made the more money they would get. The crew was like a team and everyone earned the same amount of money. All workers were expected to have skills and endurance for maximum production. It was a competition, a war where only the strong and skillful survived. If a worker was not able to keep up the pace, he would quit or be harassed by the others and be forced to quit. The job was so physical that women were very rare in the ground crews. The main part of the crew worked in *trios*[52]. Two cutters and a packer formed the trio. Each crew had three closers and four loaders. These workers earned at different rates and were considered the elite positions; the most demanding, but best paid. It was hard to be accepted in a crew. New candidates had to have a relative or friend that would teach them the trade. New workers would work without pay for a few days to practice. The first few days, the new harvesters needed support from their friends while they improve their skills. Otherwise, it would be impossible to start from scratch.

"Tu tío Pablo vendrá más tarde[53]*,"* said my father. We had not seen my uncle for a few months and we were happy he was coming with *los lechugueros*. My uncle had learned the trade and often followed the harvests in Imperial Valley, Bakersfield and Salinas. We were very happy to see my uncle; he was always nice and would take us places and give us

---

[52] Teams of three

[53] Your uncle Pablo will arrive later

money to spend. He was the only relative we had in California and we liked to stay as close as possible to him. He invited my father to learn to cut lettuce but my father refused.

"Duele mucho el cuerpo[54]," my father would say.

He argued that he had no need to suffer all the physical pain. His friends would tease him about working with the women and being lazy.

"Quédate con las mujeres guevon[55]!" They would shout at him.

My father ignored them and answered with an insult. My uncle was coming to Salinas in his car, which meant we could have more options to go places. My uncle would live in the large barracks with the other men, but he would visit us frequently. I liked to visit him. He would gather with other workers to chat. I loved to listen to their stories of greatness and boasting about the amounts of boxes they harvested in one day. It was an obsession; everyone bragged about working in a crew that packed enough boxes to fill a railroad car.

"Puro Carro Por Trío,[56]" they would brag.

Six hundred and forty boxes; it was the magic number to proclaim greatness. It was the myth of *los lechugueros*.

Fernando was very excited about their arrival. He told us how *los lechugueros* would ask the children in the camp to do some simple chores and they would pay for the help. They were always bragging about the money they made and would show off their checks when they received them. Now we would always have money to go to the Dairy Queen and buy ice cream. We always went and helped with the trash or to sweep the barrack and they would give us a dollar each every time we helped. They also offered us whatever they had: sodas, food, or candy. The workers also played games and sports after work. They played in the yard, which

---

[54] Too many body aches

[55] Stay with the women, lazy man.

[56] One train container per three men team

was used for entertainment and exercise as well as to park their cars. For us it was fun to watch; especially on weekdays, since we had nothing else to do. *Los lechugueros* were my celebrities.

"Maybe I will be a *lechuguero* one day," I thought, "and travel all over California after the harvest." I will be the best that ever existed. Maybe I can cut *"un carro por trio."*

With the arrival of my uncle, we had constant family gatherings where we enjoyed good food and drinks. Their conversations extended well into the night. I always liked to listen; I was the oldest and I was allowed to stay to some extent. School was out and we were excited about our grades. We showed them to my uncle and spoke to him in English. We tried to carry out conversations with him and my father, who could speak a little. It was good to hear them try to use English because most farm workers did not want to learn.

"Si el gringo quiere hablar conmigo que aprenda Español[57]," they would say.

There was a wide-spread feeling of resentment and rejection from the workers towards the Anglo society and not learning the language seemed to be a form of protest. Some complained about the hard work and low pay and felt they were being exploited. Some felt the farmers were getting rich with the sacrifice of the workers and their families. Many workers were conformists and expected to be farm workers all their lives. They worked in low paying jobs and at the end of the day they would isolate themselves in Mexican neighborhoods and camps where English was not necessary. There were areas in the different communities where businesses provided workers with Mexican food items, some services and entertainment: theater, holidays and dances were all Mexican style. It provided a sensation of living in their country. Interaction with the Anglo society was rare and the language barrier served as an excuse.

---

[57] If the white man needs to speak to me let him learn Spanish.

My family planned to move to another area after we finished with school. The thinning season was ending and my father did not want to try working in the lettuce harvest for now. He wanted to go find something else. My father and my uncle talked about picking fruit.

"At least we don't have to be bending over all day," my mother said. The fruit was picked using ladders and could be dangerous but my mother wanted to try it. "*Me voy a quedar jorobada*[58]," she would say laughing.

El cortito was exhausting and they could use a change. Besides, now that we were out of school it would be easier to care for us in the orchards rather than paying babysitters to care for us. It was common to have families with their children working in the orchards. The adults would pick the top fruit using ladders and the children helped gathering the fruit that fell to the ground or picked from the lower branches.

"*Los niños pueden pizcar las barbas*[59]," said my father.

To be able to travel we needed transportation and my uncle's car was having mechanical problems. My father made the decision to buy his own car even though he did not know how to drive.

"Pablo can drive it while I learn and get my driver's license," he said.

We were so happy we jumped up and down with joy.

"Do you mean we will have our own car?" we kept asking over and over. The season had been good and my mother and father had worked hard; they had saved enough money to buy the car.

"*Valió la pena la chinga*[60]," said my mother.

I remember her anguished face when I visited her en *el cortito*, but now she was happy. She felt it was worth it. We went cruising around

---

[58] I will become a hunchback

[59] The children can pick at the *beard* (The lower branches).

[60] It was worth the whipping.

[61] A station wagon.

Salinas looking for a good used car.

"*Una camioneta*[61]," said my father, "a large station wagon where we can fit everything we own."

We finally came to a used car lot where they had a large station wagon. It was a 1960 Dodge. It had three seats and the back one could be folded to serve as cargo area. It also had luggage rails on top to carry the larger baggage. We could fit with all our belongings and have space to spare. My uncle drove the station wagon around the block to test it.

"It is in good condition; the motor and transmission work just fine," said my uncle.

He knew about cars, at least more than my father. We had enough money to buy it. After a short debate and some good old bargaining with the owner, the deal was completed and we drove home in our first car. Our dreams were slowly coming true.

BARBAS DE ORO

WE LOADED OUR BELONGINGS early in the morning. Everything we owned fit; we didn't have to leave anything behind. Our car was big, perfect for traveling. Our father told us that we were going to Modesto.

"It is not too far; about three hours driving, depending on the traffic," said my uncle.

It was sad to leave Fernando; he had been a good friend.

"We will come back and visit," said my father as we started to drive away.

My father wanted to get to Modesto early in the day. He needed time to look for a house to rent. The drive was fun; there were many new and different things to see. The highway went through many hills and forests. We saw fruit-stands along the way selling apricots, peaches, pears and cherries. As we got closer to Modesto the weather began to get warmer.

"It will be hot," said my uncle, "but only in the afternoon and by then we will be off work and we can go to the river."

"¿Un río[62]?" we asked excited.

My uncle laughed. He knew we would be happy about living close

---

[62] A river?

45

to a river where we could cool off every day.

"I bet you will like it," he said. "We will have a picnic there as soon as we arrive."

My uncle stopped at a store to stretch and for a bathroom break. We bought some groceries to make a picnic at the river. My father bought a newspaper to start looking for a house to rent. We hoped to find one soon or else it meant sleeping in the car. When we got to the river, my brother, sister, and I started down the grassy hill towards the bank under the caution of my mother, who worried about how deep the river was.

"It is not dangerous," my uncle said.

The river was sandy and shallow and the current was mild. We took off our shoes and went in knee deep; we just wanted to feel the water. We changed our clothes after we ate the sandwiches my mother had prepared while my father and uncle looked in the newspaper for a house to rent. My father and uncle went to see an advertised house that was not too far away. We stayed with my mother to play in the river and its park. "This is wonderful," we all agreed. The park had everything a child would want. There was the river with a sandy bank where children could build castles and mountains or cover themselves with the sand. To one side there were picnic areas with grills and benches. To the other side there was a great playground with all kinds of equipment: swings, see-saws merry-go-rounds, monkey bars, and slides. My favorite was a huge slide with a curve and a bump, and ending in a sandy pit. I must have slid twenty times before my father and uncle came with good news: they had found a nice house to rent a few blocks away from the river. It was old, but it had many rooms. The children would have their own room and there were two more bedrooms for the adults. The house also had a large kitchen area and a living room where we could put our television, which we were able to keep thanks to our huge station wagon. The house was furnished, so we did not have to visit the local flea market to buy anything. My mother would joke about going to the local flea market for enjoyment and not for the need. The best thing was that we could return to the river again. We would live close by. For now, it was time to go.

It was the apricot season; there were many orchards around Modesto. The fresh air with the apricot fragrance was unique and never experienced by us before.

"*Hmm, qué bonito aroma*[63]," my mother repeated over and over.

As we walked inside the orchard my father picked a few ripe apricots and handed them to us.

"Here, taste, not even the rich people can do this," he said laughing. "They buy the fruit at the store, bruised and refrigerated. The fruit loses its real taste."

The apricot my father had given me was the most beautiful I had ever seen: large, firm, juicy, sweet, and cooled by the chill of the morning. It was delicious.

"This is an experience only farm workers can have," bragged my father.

My uncle had been to this orchard before and knew where to look for the foreman. We soon found the crew among the trees. After talking the terms and procedures of the job, we were hired. Working in the orchard was convenient since we were able to drive our car to the set of trees assigned to us. My mother and father could work and watch the children. My sister and I would help care for our younger siblings and my mother would only intervene when necessary. The crew was mostly families with children; there were few single harvesters. Each family formed their own small crew; all the members helped in some way. The younger ones were mainly babysitters that would do their best to entertain their baby brothers and sisters. They would alert the

47

parents if something needed their attention. The older children helped with the harvesting of the fruit. Sometimes, even the smaller ones would go and lift the fallen fruit as part of a game that parents encouraged as they began to teach the children the trade. Older children would start carrying a bucket with a strap hanging from the shoulder and neck to pick the fruit off the lower branches. The fruit was placed in boxes stacked at the end of the tree set where it was inspected, counted and registered to each family's account. The families would get paid at a set rate for every box they picked during the day.

Fruit harvesting requires special skills. The most important was how to carry and set the ladder in positions to reach the most fruit. All the ripe fruit had to be picked. Workers were reprimanded if they left fruit on the trees. Going up and down the ladder is exhausting and requires good conditioning. The weather was cool in the morning, but later it would get hot, and inside the orchard with little airflow, it would really get uncomfortable.

"*¡Barbas de oro!¡ Barbas de oro[64]!*" shouted of some of the workers as it got hotter.

My uncle said that it was a way the harvesters called the wind to blow and make it cool. The object was to pick the fruit and pick it as fast as possible; the more you picked the more money you earned. I loved to see the technique of the champion harvesters.

"*Parecen changos[65],*" said my mother as we saw them climb the ladders among the braches. I was impressed and wanted to be like them. Everyone teased me saying I would be a very small *chango*. I was so determined to learn that I asked the foreman for a small ladder, one I could carry. I might not be able to reach all the fruit from the tall trees but I could help get more of the lower branches and pick some off the

---

[64] Golden Beard! Golden Beard!

[65] They look like monkeys.

smaller trees. The man was so impressed with my initiative and desire to learn that he promised to bring one the next day. I told my mother about it and she warned me to be careful. They encouraged it because they knew I had the potential to learn the trade and help the family earn more money.

The following day the foreman called me and said he had a surprise for me. It was fourteen-step ladder, much smaller than the rest. It was heavy but I had enough strength to carry it and with practice I would be able to move it at will. Soon I was climbing to high branches and helping fill boxes faster than many of the slower adults. Whenever I had a chance, I would politely question the champions about their skills and they gladly gave me many tips. Gradually I became better and better. My mother and father were very happy, and at gatherings, they received many compliments from their friends.

"*Tu hijo es muy trabajador,*[66]" they would say.

My father would brag that I inherited his traits. "Just like his father," he would say teasing over and over. "*Trabajador como su padre*[67]".

As I gained confidence, I looked for opportunities to climb the bigger ladders. When my mother was resting, tending to the children, or preparing our food and her ladder was set where there was fruit, I would climb to get it. The larger ladders could take you to the top of the tallest trees. It was a challenge to climb so high. There was nothing to hold on to, just your balance and staying calm, not being afraid. The sight was beautiful, like being on top of clouds formed by the treetops. You could hear the people singing, chatting, joking, and laughing, trying to cheer themselves through a hard day's work. But the cry of a child echoing through the orchard, asking for their mothers, for food, or expressing their desire to go home, portrayed the great sacrifice the families endured

---

[66] Your son is a hard worker.

[67] Hard worker like his father.

to subsist. At the top, you could hear noises, but not see anything but a carpet of green with monumental mountains in the background.

"That's were the wind comes from when the harvesters called it," I thought. "*Barbas de oro! Barbas de oro!*, I shouted as loud as I could.

I felt a light breeze.

"*¡Barbas de oro*"! *¡Barbas de oro!*," I insisted.

Then I felt it, a cool breeze blowing in my face, refreshing, caressing me as to reward my accomplishment. Perhaps that was the sign, letting me know I was considered a true *pizcador*[68]. It was an exciting moment interrupted by my mother, who concerned for my safety, shouted; "*¡Bajaté de ahí! Te vas a dar un madrazo bien dado, muchacho*[69]".

I climbed down and went to gather with the rest of the family who was getting ready to eat the sandwiches prepared by my mother. I liked to eat at the orchard. It was like a picnic. We always took different things to prepare our meals. We kept them in an ice chest my father had bought at the local *pulga*. We always had sodas and water to last all day long. We would spread blankets on the ground and lay down to stretch and rest our aching bodies as we ate. You could hear the other families doing the same. Among the trees you could hear the lament of tired workers and the cries of children begging to go home, and then silence. Everyone ate quietly. After a few minutes the chatting between workers continued, intermingled with laughter and singing, as if the people had recuperated their energy and their desire to continue working, to persist with their struggle to fill as many boxes as possible.

Sometimes after work we would immediately go to the river and just re-supply the ice chest with food for the rest of the day. At the time we stopped working, the weather was very hot and we did not have an air cooler, so we'd rather play in the coolness of the river and its park. My

---

[68] Fruit harvester

[69] Get down from there, you will have a bad fall.

mother would come to the river with us as my father and uncle would lay on the grass talking, usually about returning to *Guadalajara*[70]. It was my fathers dream to raise enough money to buy a house in Guadalajara and never come back to *"el Norte"*. My father was learning to drive and was planning to get his drivers license soon; he wanted to raise enough money to go. We all wanted to go. Our entire family lived there and we had not seen them in several years. It would be great if we could go and tell everyone everything we knew about el Norte[71].

At first they were only murmurs, then the voices got louder. My mother and father were fighting again. My father had a drinking problem and my mother hated to see him drunk. She would complain that he wasted money we could use to buy things we needed, or save to go to Guadalajara. He would raise the tone of his voice to intimidate her. It was his technique to get her off his case, an emotional black mail. He knew his loudness would wake us up and my mother worried we would hear the insults he used against her.

"This is how you met me! Why do you complain now?" he would ask. *"El hombre debe ser macho*[72]*."*

A phrase I often heard from many Mexican farm workers. A myth integrated in to the culture about male dominance and female submissiveness, el *machismo*.

"I am not going to be under the skirt of a woman, *hay que ser macho*[73]," he mumbled, as my uncle intervened in defense of my mother. He was awakened by the shouts and angrily, scolded my father. My uncle was the oldest and demanded respect for the family. My father stormed out threatening to never come back. He always returned after a few beers, lay

---

[70] Mexican city

[71] The North

[72] A man is supposed to be bad.

[73] Lets be a man.

on the couch, and slept with loud snores that could be heard all through the house.

My mother was very quiet the next day as she prepared our food and got us ready for work. My father woke complaining about his hangover and drank lots of cold water.

"Ahhhh!" he exclaimed" and added up. "It tastes better than beer." He complained all day as if he wanted us to feel sorry for his suffering.

"*Que te lleve la chingada*[74]," would mumble my mother.

She was very upset and wishing my father the worse hangover ever to pay for his actions. By the end of the day, they would be talking, and soon, it would all be forgotten, a behavior pattern my siblings and I learned to live with for many years.

I looked outside the window and saw my father driving the station wagon up the driveway. It was so clean; it looked like a white bird, a beautiful dove. We had seen it full of dirt from the orchards for so many days that we had forgotten what color it was.

"*La pasaste? La pasaste*[75]?" we asked my father, as we ran outside jumping and shouting. He had gone to take his driving test and we all hoped he had passed it. He bragged about passing it easily.

"What do you think? Don't you see me driving? And I did not get it with green stamps[76]," he would tease, happy about his accomplishment.

---

[74] Go to hell

[75] Did you pass?

[76] Stamps that were given in stores as a reward for a purchase; they could be exchanged for prices.

MI TIERRA

WE WERE ALL HAPPY. It meant we would begin our journey to Guadalajara, *mi tierra*[77]. The journey would be difficult. Guadalajara was very far and it was the first time my father would drive for such a long trip. He was used to short drives to the store or to work. On some occasions he drove on the freeway to practice, but now, it was the real thing. He knew it was a great challenge and he was very concerned about the family's safety; so many cars and large trucks. He planned the trip carefully. He wanted to avoid the traffic in Los Angeles so we left in the afternoon to navigate the great city at night. The trip would be in two stages: from Modesto to Mexicali and from Mexicali to Guadalajara. In Mexicali, we would rest for two days and fix our tourist documents and permits in order to travel in Mexico by car.

"Now we have green cards," my father would tease. "The law requires that we have permits or else we would face many problems."

My father would be the only driver, since my uncle Pablo would not go with us. He was going further north to the pear harvest. He gave my father some advice.

"*Nomás vete por la primera línea y no te salgas hasta que llegues*[78]," he

---

[77] My land

[78] Just go on the first lane and stay in it until you get there.

would say laughing, teasing my father.

The first part of the trip was nerve wracking. My father became intimidated by the heavy traffic and demanded complete silence. We could see the stress on his face as he struggled to calm himself. Any noise he heard he would jump up, slow down, and ask that we looked around to see if we were missing a tire or some other piece of the car. He drove so slowly. To my disappointment, all the cars and trucks passed him. Even the very old men drove faster and eventually overtook us. The old drivers Don Juanito usually bypassed turned to look in dismay, wondering if we had a mechanical problem or needed help. Every bump we hit, my father would mumble, hoping nothing was wrong. When the big trucks passed us, producing a strong gust and causing our car to swerve, he would clinch to the steering wheel as hard as he could to control the car. My mother would mumble or shout insults at the drivers and demanded silence. She told everyone to be alert for the maniacs driving around us. My father blamed our talking for distracting him and making him nervous. He wanted us instead to look out for big trucks, and when one approached we would tell him so he'd be prepared to control the car against the strong gust. "We have to be safe," was the phrase he repeated over and over. I kept looking for the trucks and warning him. There were so many, hundreds, and all of them passed us. I hoped we would find one that was so slow that my father would pass it. I wanted a victory; we have to pass at least one. My father has a license and deserves to win at least one time. It was not to be. He drove like my uncle had advised him, on the first lane all the way. I don't remember my uncle saying to go so slow, but my father did, perhaps breaking a record of not passing a single car for six hundred miles.

The drive to Guadalajara was better. The road was narrow, only two lanes, but the traffic was extremely light for most of the way. Sometimes it was very lonely. It was fortunate if you came by a vehicle of any kind.

Occasionally, large buses would overtake us, intimidating my father. The trucks were slow, giving my father an opportunity to practice passing a vehicle. I felt great when he finally decided to do it.

"OK! Hang on!" he said. "*Voy a pasar a esta pinchi tortuga, nada mas pa que vean que tan chingon soy pa manejar.*[79]"

My father laughed nervously, bragging about his achievement and of being a great driver. From then on, my father drove a little faster and we had several victories along the long trip to Guadalajara.

We had traveled to Guadalajara by train before. It was the first time we made the trip by car. There were many interesting things to see in the populated areas along the way. People and animals were common, crossing the highway, something we never saw in California. Sometimes we had to stop in the middle of the highway to let them cross. In Los Angeles my father had urged us to warn him about huge trucks, here we had to warn him about cows and goats. We stopped in several small towns to get food and gas, and after a long day of driving, we stopped to rest first in *Hermosillo, Sonora*, and the next day in *Mazatlan, Sinaloa*. Both stops were part of my father's plan. My siblings and I were curious about the way people spoke in those areas. They sounded very funny and we would tease each other, imitating their tone of voice as we talked.

"*Qiubule vale. Buenos días patroncito*[80]," we mimic.

"That is how people speak around here," my mother explained.

We asked my mother if this was the way they spoke in Guadalajara. She agreed, but warned us that it was contagious. She said that eventually we would speak like that, too, after a few days.

"The children here also think you speak funny yourselves. They might be making fun of you right now, joking about how strange kids

---

[79] I am going to pass this damn turtle to show you how bad I am driving.

[80] Greetings of hello and good morning with regional words; friend (vale), Boss (patroncito).

from California speak," my mother said teasing us, imitating how we spoke. "*Simón, ese, pásame la soda plis*[81]."

Finally, after two days and one night, we arrived at the great city of Guadalajara. All of us had been born in or around this city except for my brother Rafael, who was born in Mexicali. During the trip my mother and father told us stories of how we had come to this world. I was born during a storm in a tent house and my mother was tended by a *partera*[82]. The tent had to be held down so the wind would not take it. My father was out drinking and my grandfather had gone after him, and forcing him to come. I was born on Mexican Mother's Day, May 10th, and forever teased about being a *Madrecita*[83]. They said it was the reason I was born short in stature.

"*Por eso naciste una madrecita*[84]," my friends teased me.

In a sense I was lucky. No one would forget my birthday since Mother's Day is a very popular celebration. My mother would tell me tenderly that I was the best Mother's Day present she had ever received. I was named after my paternal grandfather, Lucio, who was very happy I was born. At that time, I was the only male left in the Padilla family. My other uncles, Pablo and Jesus, had only daughters and they would acquire another name once they married. I was the only male left to continue with the Padilla heritage. I still remember how my grandfather, proudly, would take me horse riding around the streets of *Tototlán*, a small town where he had a small farm. He was very popular with women and liked to ride his horse *Viento*[85] to impress them.

---

[81] Yes, dude, give me the soda please.

[82] Mid wife

[83] Little mother

[84] That is why you were born a small mother.

[85] Wind

My grandfather would tell me, "*Mira mijo puras viejas bombas*[86]," he would laugh with me as we rode *Viento* away.

"*Son bombas abuelo*[87]?" I would ask.

"*Si mijo,*[88]" he would say. "They are all worn out," and laughed out loud, pointing out. One day we were riding, he flirted with a group of women, greeting them.

"*Hola señoritas, buenos días*[89]," he introduced me to them, "*es mi nieto*[90]."

The women smiled and told each other how cute I was.

Unexpectedly, I answered, "*Vámonos abuelo, son puras viejas bombas.*"

Embarrassed, my grandfather's face turned red. He apologized and rode away immediately. I had no idea it was an insult. I had called them "worn out women" just like my grandfather, but I did not know I was not supposed to say it in front of them. Later, my grandfather joked about my action as something expected from a man.

"*Mijo va ser un verdadero macho*[91]," my grandfather would say.

My father had a good time remembering the incidents my grandfather lived with me the last four years of his life.

My parents did not have much education. My father did not finish high school and my mother only went to third grade. They lived in a tent and my father milked cows for a living on the outskirts of Guadalajara. He told stories of how he would sink me in the milk containers naked and bathe me with milk. He wanted me to be healthy and strong to

---

[86] Look son they are bombs. It is an idiomatic expression meaning worn out women.

[87] They are bombs (wornout) grandfather?

[88] Yes, son.

[89] Hello, ladies, good morning.

[90] My grandson

[91] My son will be a real man.

face life. My mother would say that maybe I had *"un accidente, o dos[92]"* while I was submerged. We wondered who drank the milk afterwards and pitied them. My father did not have a good future in Guadalajara, and the myth of the American Dream aroused his curiosity to go to California. I would hear his conversations with my mother.

"I will come and get you soon. I will get a good job and send you money," he would tell her. "Soon we will be together en *El Norte*. My uncle grew up under similar circumstances and was already living up north. They both were able to cross *de mojados* [93]and later acquired legal residence. The family that stayed behind in Guadalajara was well off; they had property and jobs with a future. *El Norte* was not appealing to them.

"*No le pedimos nada al Norte[94]*," they said, and boasted about not needing to be *emigrados[95]*.

Our relatives lived well in their beloved land, México, but they resented that two members of their family would go and sell themselves to the *Gringos*. My uncle and father did not listen and ventured to the border despite the family's protests. On the border, they found a way to cross and found work and housing. Many illegal people had contacts to help them settle. My father had my uncle Pablo. My father and uncle emigrated looking for their destiny and the American Dream.

We finally arrived in Guadalajara.

"We will stay with your aunt *Lupe*," my father had said.

It was the house that served as refuge for all the relatives. It was big, with an inside patio and five bedrooms adjacent around the perimeter. It had a large, open receiving room and a closed living room. The

---

[92] One accident or two

[93] wetbacks

[94] We do not ask the north for anything.

[95] immigrants

kitchen and dining room had space to serve a large group. Big meals were common; my aunt always offered her home to relatives from other areas when they came to Guadalajara on business or to attend school. They received us with a warm welcome, cheering, hugging us, and asking about the trip. As we unloaded our luggage, I noticed people looking out windows and doors at us. They were all curious about the people from *el Norte* that had just arrived. Some came out of their homes to witness the reception. I had lived my first four years in that neighborhood before my father took us to California, so I knew some of the kids. I wondered if they still lived there. I would love to play with them again.

The family was happy we were visiting, but we could feel bitterness. *Mi tía* [96] criticized everything we mentioned about California and labeled us as "Gringo wanna-be's."

"*Se van a convertir en gringos con los ojos azules y el pelo güero*[97]," she warned us.

She also criticized how we spoke and discouraged us from using the *gringo* words that formed part of the border language we were acquiring, *Spanglish.*

"You don't say soda, parqueadero, o breca," my aunt would correct us. "*Se dice refresco, estacionamiento y freno*[98]."

Our relatives would correct us and chide, saying that we were Mexican with a *nopal*[99] on our foreheads that could not be removed.

"*El nopal ni quien se los quite*[100]," they would tell us. "Even if you speak English you will still be Mexican," they would add sarcastically.

The reception from my mother's family was more passionate. They

---

[96] My aunt

[97] You Will Turn Into Americans With Blue Eyes And Blond Hair.

[98] You Say Soda, Parking Lot And Brake.

[99] Cactus

[100] No One Can Rid You Of That Cactus

lived in small *ranchos*[101] raising animals and working the land. They had a strong desire to go to California, but, they did not have the resources to make the trip; they were jealous of our success. They also criticized us about *El Norte* but deep inside they wished they were as lucky as us. My sister and I did not respond to their harassment. We knew this was not the place to play our game of speaking English; we would have to postpone it for some other time. It was obvious it was not welcomed.

For most of our stay in Guadalajara my father was out drinking. He loved to be in a *cantina*[102] with his friends getting drunk and boasting about *El Norte*. He would spend hours telling exaggerated stories of how easy it was to earn dollars.

"*Recoges los dólares fácil*[103]!" he would say.

We just listened quietly. My father wanted to give the impression that we had found The American Dream. Deep inside we wanted to believe it too, but it was far from happening. His sisters and nieces would tell my father to stay away from drinking but he had no intention to listen to reason. My mother knew my father would get drunk but she ignored it. She was determined to enjoy the trip.

"*Si se emborracha mejor*[104]," she would say, resigned to her destiny. "That way we don't have to deal with him."

My mother learned to make the best of life with her children.

---

[101] Ranch

[102] bar

[103] You pick up dollars easily!

[104] It's better if he gets drunk.

RETURN TO EL NORTE

It was great to return to *El Norte*[105]. We felt relieved when we were allowed to cross the border after showing our green cards to the officer.

"*De donde ser ustedes*[106]?" he asked in his funny Spanish.

"From Guadalajara," my father answered.

After the officer checked our luggage, he let us through. We were thankful we had returned safely. We felt joy driving on the streets of Calexico once again. There was a certain feeling of security we had not experienced in a long time in Guadalajara. We felt good to return to this small town in the middle of the desert. My father said we would stay for a few months until the fruit harvest started further north. My father had rented a small apartment in the same area where we had lived the first time we crossed the border, close to the park where we had so much fun playing. The most exciting part was returning to Rockwood, our first school. It would be great to see our first friends and teachers in California. We were anxious for our parents to enroll us in school. We looked forward to attending English class with Mr. Lopez and practicing our vocabulary. Now my sister and I could play our English speaking

---

[105] The North

[106] Where do you come from?

game we had missed so much during our stay in Guadalajara.

I was now in the fourth grade. My sister and I had missed school because of our trip. Now we worked hard to catch up. We adapted well to our new teachers. Some of the students from the previous year were in our class, making it easier for us to integrate. Mr. Lopez gave us a warm welcome when we went to his class early in the morning. He spoke to us in English, testing us to see how much vocabulary we had acquired. He was impressed at our determination to learn the language. It was common for migrant students to fall behind in school intimidated by the language barrier and the constant moving after the crop harvest. He continued to encourage us, and soon he would not speak or allow us to speak Spanish in class. Rockwood was more tolerant than other schools we attended about letting students speak Spanish. It was prohibited but not strictly enforced compared to what we had experienced in schools further north.

During our stay in Calexico, my parents worked *en el cortito*[107] and harvested a variety of vegetables. My father did not like this work and always complained that harvesting fruit was better.

"Soon we will go to Tulare, California," he would tell my mother.

My father had a friend that invited us to go live there and promised my father to help him settle down. In the mean time, my parents would work in Imperial Valley harvesting: broccoli, cauliflower, and mustard, until the orange harvest started in Tulare. Our cousin Sara would come from Guadalajara to visit in California and would stay with us for some time. She came to help care for us while my mother and father worked. It sounded like a good plan and my mother supported it, but my sister and I did not like the idea of moving to an unknown place; it would mean starting over in a strange place. God knows what would await us there.

---

[107] Short hoe

It was raining so hard we could hardly see the road. My father was very tense and kept complaining about the difficulty of driving under such conditions. Again, we had started the trip to Tulare early so we would have daylight to look for a place to rent. My father's friend, Francisco, had offered his home for us to stay for a few days until we settled down, but my mother insisted we look for our own place.

"*El muerto y el arrimado apesta a los dos días*[108]," my mother would say. My father insisted that this man was a very close childhood friend.

"We are just like family," he argued.

My mother refused to listen and said that even if his friend had good intentions we would become a burden for his family after a few days.

Francisco welcomed us warmly. He invited us in and introduced his family. His wife looked Mexican but did not speak Spanish, or at least that is what she said.

"*Yo hablando muy poquito*, little *Español*," she said to excuse herself.

They had a daughter about my sister's age, eight years old, who also spoke only English. Their house had three bedrooms, a large living room, a kitchen and dining room. Outside was a large yard with trees and swings. We could not go out because of the rain, so the children watched television while the adults engaged in long conversations.

"It has been raining very hard for many days," explained Francisco.

It was impossible to work. Everyone was hoping it would clear soon or the fruit would be damaged and everyone would suffer. Extremely rainy seasons could not be predicted but it was a farm worker's feared since working in the fields depended on the climate condition. The weather could damage the crops and it was the farmers and farm workers who would suffer the consequences.

For a week, we stayed in Francisco's house. My parents slept in the

---

[108] Visitors and the dead stink after two days.

63

guest room with Maria Luisa, my baby sister. The rest of us (our cousin Sara, my brother Rafael, my sister Silvia, and I) slept on the floor, in the living room. During the day we stayed away as much as possible looking for a house we could afford to rent, or just passing time to avoid being a burden for Francisco and his family. My mother was right; Francisco's wife treated us coldly as the days went by, and we were not comfortable. When we were house searching we would buy items to make sandwiches to eat at the park. We usually stayed in the car because of the rain. It would not stop and we wondered if it was ever going to stop. One day, as we were wondering, we saw an abandoned house within a pomegranate orchard. It did not have a sign, but we stopped to ask, hoping we could rent it. A man came out from a nearby house when he saw us approach. My father, with his limited English, asked about renting the house. The man explained that it had been abandoned for a long time and that it was not fit to live in. My father desperately insisted trying to convince the man. He even lied about having been living in the car for a few days. He promised we would be there only for a few days until we found a suitable place. The man hesitantly agreed. He told my father he would make some repairs so that at least it would protect us from the environment. The house was big and had several rooms but was missing the back door and a few windows.

"We will be fine," said my mother. "We will cover them with cardboard until they are repaired." She was happy that we would not have to stay in Francisco's home anymore, invading his privacy. We thanked Francisco for his hospitality. He continued to offer his help and offered my father some money. My father reluctantly accepted and told him that we would pay back as soon as possible. Francisco smiled and told us not to worry and let out a sight of relief as he saw us leave. We packed our things and went to clean the house to make it more appealing. It would take a lot of work to get rid of the dust and the insects that ran all over in protest of our invasion of their home. The house had a few old mattresses and furniture stored in one of the rooms. We took them out and pounded on them with a stick to remove as much dust as possible. Spiders and scorpions began crawling out, only to be squashed by my mother's broom.

"We have to kill them all now or they will get us later," she said as she inspected every inch of the mattresses.

It took us several hours to make them suitable for use. During the next few days we would have to work hard to make as many improvements as possible. We made many improvements in order to upgrade it to look like other cabins we had lived in before. For us it was our new castle.

On our first night, my siblings and I were exploring the house while my parents made plans for the next day. They were hoping for a break on the weather so that they could work in the orange harvest to earn enough money to get out of this difficult situation. Suddenly, we heard a knock on the front door, the only door the house had. We wonder whom it could be since Francisco did not know where the house was and we did not know anyone else. We heard a loud voice in English telling us to open the door and announcing they were from The Emigration Department. We were startled; we did not expect these kinds of guests.

"*Es la migra*[109]!" said my mother, intimidated by the sudden visit.

"*Creen que somos mojados*[110]," said my father, as he opened the door.

One officer was standing on the front door as three others were surrounding the house. They all had their hands resting on their guns as if getting ready to draw them if needed. The officer asked my father for our documents and stepped in the house, cautiously looking around. The rest of the officers came in cautiously through the back door. We were startled by the sudden visit. My siblings and I gather around my

---

[109] It is the immigration officers

[110] They think we are wetbacks.

mother; the emigration raid had frightened us. The officers' approach was out of a dramatic movie. It's OK said my father, trying to explain to the officers we were legal residents. My mother searched through her purse for our *micas*[111], to show the officers. My father and cousin Sara did the same. Trembling, my mother handed the officer the *micas*.

"*Somos emigrados, están nuevecitas*[112]," she tried to explain.

The officers returned the documents and coldly told us that they had a report about illegal people living here, but that the papers seemed to be in order. They mumbled something among themselves, walked out of the house, got in their vehicles, and left.

"*Pinches Gringos nos reportaron como mojados*[113]," my mother cussed.

It rained all night; we could hear it pouring on the roof. The weather and the tense moments with *la migra* made us all uneasy. I could hear my mother and father whispering, but could not understand what they were saying. They worried about the uncertainty of our situation. Money and food were running low and if the rain did not stop soon we would be in a desperate situation. Coming in search of the orange harvest had been a misfortune.

The next day my parents did not work because of the rain and took my sister and me to a nearby school. On the way we had a chance to see the neighborhood. All the houses where huge and beautiful, surrounded by trees and large lawns, complete with beautiful cars parked in their large driveways. The school was the best we had seen up to now. It had beautiful classrooms and a large playground with many games and equipment. All the students were neatly dressed in beautiful clothes. The secretary looked at us as being out of place. We dressed in shabby clothes and she seemed surprised, as if wondering about our presence.

---

[111] Green card or identification card

[112] We are naturalized, they are brand new.

[113] Damn Anglos, they reported us as wetbacks.

The secretary hesitated for a few seconds and asked what we wanted.

"My children come to school," said my father proudly, in his limited English and strong accent.

With a confused look on her face, the secretary went into an office while my father wondered if she had understood. After a few minutes she came back asking us for proof of residency. She questioned the fact that we lived in that area and our legal residency. She tried to explain that perhaps we did not belong to that school that only residents of that neighborhood could register. My father showed proof of residency but the secretary insisted that there had to be a mistake. I helped my father answer many questions. Finally, after reviewing all our documents, we were reluctantly accepted. We did not understand why they were objecting to our enrollment, but it made us feel out of place. Their attitude made me uneasy; I felt rejected. They probably wondered how a bunch of ragged Mexicans had been able to obtain proof of residency there. They did not know we lived in the only abandoned house in the area.

I was very nervous when I was escorted to my classroom. I followed with butterflies in my stomach and my head bowed down, intimidated by the environment. My knees trembled as I waited at the classroom door while the woman who escorted me whispered to the teacher. As they talked, the teacher glanced at me stone faced, nodding her head. I felt the stare of the students and heard their murmurs. I dared not look up. From the corner of my eye, I saw the students, all neatly dressed. I felt ashamed at my torn shoes and old clothes. I wanted to run away as far as I could. Instead, I just stood there waiting, wondering how my sister was doing. I knew she was going through the same situation. The teacher approached me and asked me for my name.

"*Lucio Padilla,*" I answered.

"*Lushio Padila,*" she tried to repeat mispronouncing my name and making the class laugh. I nodded and tried to smile, hoping I could get a positive reaction from the teacher. I did not. Her expression never changed. She pointed at an empty desk and told me to sit as she proceeded with her lesson.

During recess, I stood lonely in an isolated part of the playground looking around hoping to see my sister. I knew I wouldn't since she came out at a different time. No one came to me and I was afraid to approach any students, fearing rejection. I tried to be brave and take the initiative.

Maybe if I prove myself by showing I'm a good student I can blend in, I thought.

The games the students were playing were the same as the ones I had learned in the other schools: four squares, tetherball, and kick ball. Maybe if I showed them I was good at playing these games some students would accept me. I thought about it, but I cowered still intimidated by the cold reception. It was so different from the experience I had in other schools I had attended.

After recess we returned to the class and continued with the math class, my favorite subject. I gathered courage and participated with enthusiasm. I did well but I did not impress anyone. Instead I was called a show-off by some of the students. The teacher was not impressed either. She favored other students and down played my ability in math by limiting my participation. Again, I felt rejected and my anxiety increased. Again, I felt the desire to run away and never come back. I felt like crying, but I was not about to give these people the satisfaction of seeing me defeated. I comforted myself by thinking about my mother's words.

"Try hard and don't do anything that would get you in trouble," she told me.

During lunch, I sat quietly eating as fast as I could and planning how I would try to join a game. Maybe I could make some friends while playing. After being dismissed, I ran to the four squares and lined up, waiting for my turn. Students angrily told me to go away.

"Get away you dirty greaser. We don't want you here," one student told me, obviously trying to hurt my feelings.

I had never been called a dirty greaser. I did not know the meaning of their insult but the expression was enough to understand. I tried to ignore it. I continued to look for a square where I was allowed to play. Finally, I found one where some older students were playing. They were mostly fifth and sixth graders and they wanted the satisfaction of embarrassing me by beating me badly. At last I got the chance to play. I was noticeably superior and they started to accuse me of cheating. All of them wanted the chance to knock me off the square. The bigger students began to harass me with insults and occasional shoving as they went near me. They teamed up to knock me out from the game, but they failed, and I continued to disqualify every one, making them angry. The bell rang and everyone began the walk back to the class. I was satisfied that I had defeated everyone, even the older students. It was a great feeling of achievement. But, I was the only one happy about it; everybody else left in discontent, continuing to argue that I had cheated.

In the next two days the situation in the school escalated. Students were rude and the teacher rejected me. I was confused. In the other schools, I was successful at getting friends. In this school everyone was angry with me. The teacher never changed her demeanor and saw me as an undesirable student. She never showed appreciation for my good behavior and participation. Despite the disadvantages, I always gave my best effort and try to excel in class. On the playground, I tried hard to adapt, but to no avail. The aggression increased, particularly by a large sixth grader who was upset he could not defeat me in any of the games. He was the school bully and always harassed me. He tried to intimidate me with name-calling and by shoving me at every chance he had. I was not afraid, but I tried to avoid him, thinking about my mother's words telling me *"pórtate, bien[114],"* asking me to behave and not cause problems. But as the days went by, it was getting difficult to comply with my mother's requests. The abusive behavior of some of the students was becoming unbearable. One day, after disqualifying the bully from a four square game, he pushed me so hard that I fell on the pavement and causing me a scraped elbow. I stood up and tried to ignore it, but the bully continued pushing me, calling me chicken! He made clacking noises simulating a chicken as part of the teasing. He pushed me again, this time making me fall on my butt. I was so angry that I forgot about my mother's advice. I got up, made a fist, and punched the bully in the face, busting his nose and mouth. Blood began to flow and stained his clothes. When he saw the blood, he began to cry like a baby and ran to the closest yard duty aid to complain. At that moment, I knew I was in deep trouble.

The rain stopped and my parents were able to work. The worst had passed and we had survived the difficult times. There were occasions when we had to eat oranges to ease our hunger. We were fortunate my parents were working in the orange harvest because we usually had a large reserve of this delicious fruit. We would make orange juice and fruit cocktail to compliment our meals made of beans, potatoes, eggs, and tortillas. My sister, brother, and I would usually get the largest oranges to peel and eat while we played *lotería[115]*, or cards with our cousin Sara. Since I was suspended from school and my sister was afraid to go back, we had plenty of time to play. Our experience in school was intimidating and we begged our parents not to send us again. Under the circumstances, my parents planned to move again in search of better

---

[114] Behave well.

[115] Lottery

opportunities. Our experience at school and the lack of work gave us few options. A friend of my father's had invited us to move across the mountains to King City, a small town in the Salinas Valley. The area was famous for growing large quantities of carrots and tomatoes as well as other crops, including lettuce. We were to work for Meyer Tomatoes Company, a large grower and harvester. My father said there was plenty of work and the company offered housing for the families. It seemed like a good offer and we were all eager to go as soon as possible and we did.

THE WIND

THE WIND WAS BLOWING very hard, causing our car to shake as we turned off the highway and into a small road. We crossed the railroad tracks and started up a hill. The Meyer Camp was at the top of the steep hill overlooking the small town. It was a spooky place. The camp resembled an old fortress from the medieval times. Its perimeter was formed by old barracks. A row of small, rundown shacks for families outlined one side and across a large yard there were a few large barracks to house single men, usually lettuce harvesters. The other two sides were formed by the communal kitchens and diners. Across the yard were the bathrooms. We got off the car to stretch while my father made the arrangements to get our cabin. The wind almost knocked us down. It was so strong that it forced us to seek for shelter. My father's friend said the weather was windy year round, but we would get used to it. We sarcastically refer to it as the land where people could never keep their hair combed.

The hill around the camp was full of tall, dry brush which housed many animals, including moles, rabbits, lizards, and snakes. At the bottom of the hill, were a packing shed and the main office of Joe Maggio. It was the largest crop grower in the area. They packed mainly carrots but also harvested peppers and lettuce. Next to the shed was a small river. Across the river was a family camp where the workers of *la Maggio* lived. The camp was appealing; it had well kept cabins surrounded by grassy yards. We asked our father about moving to that camp. He told us that it was only for families who worked for that company. My mother tried to console us by saying that we would one day get a house in that camp. We hurried to unload our things and settle in our new house. It felt good to have a place to protect us from the terrible wind.

King City was small agricultural town with a large Mexican population that doubled in size during the peak of harvest. San Lorenzo School was severely impacted by the phenomenon of the farm workers' migration. The largest ethnic group was Mexican farm workers who lived mainly on the east side or in highly concentrated labor camps. The Anglo population was mainly farmers, businessmen, and professionals living northwest or in nearby farms. During the school year, both groups were integrated in the same schools without incident. The school culture was adaptable to the needs of the farm workers' children. The environment dissipated our fear of school which was acquired thanks to our past experiences. We adapted rapidly; my sister and I made friends with classmates living in the same camp. We played together during recess and socialized at home daily. Our most common activity was to seek refuge from the wind in one of the communal diners and listen to the two hours of Spanish music played on the local radio station. The town provided some basic services and entertainment for the farm workers living in King City, nearby towns, camps and farms. There was a theater that showed Mexican movies on Wednesdays and English ones on Saturday and Sunday. There were services in Spanish at the main church. A fair came to town during the summer and local business sponsored weekly dances at the fairgrounds where famous Hispanic groups came to play for the exhausted farm workers. There was also a hospital, a Safe Way, a department store, a large market, a few other shops, and many *cantinas*. The bars were very popular and many farm workers, like my father, spent much of their money getting drunk there in the afternoon or on weekends.

THE CYCLE

MOST FARM WORKER FAMILIES followed a similar pattern. They made arrangements to provide care for their young while the older kids would fend for themselves or rely on older siblings to prepare for school. Some jobs allowed for families to take their children to work on weekends, holidays or summer vacation. Large families took advantage of these opportunities and saved the money to pay for childcare. The older children could help with the harvest yielding extra income. This trend went on for the duration of the harvest season. At the end, families would move to other areas where a new harvest would provide jobs. Many of the families in King City returned to Imperial Valley to continue with the crop cycle. They would work spring and summer in King City and fall and winter in Imperial Valley. The migration made sense; both areas experienced severe shortages of work and extreme contrasting weather during the off seasons. Imperial Valley had record-breaking summers with temperatures of up to 125 degrees Fahrenheit while King City had a relentless rainy season. My family made our base in Imperial Valley, as close as possible to the border. Nostalgia developed in our long stays up north; it made our returns to Imperial Valley enjoyable. We liked to live in King City but we considered Imperial Valley our home. It was a convenient pattern for my family to follow. It repeated for many years to come.

My father and mother worked together for the first years, *en el cortito* or harvesting vegetables. My uncle insisted that my father learn to harvest lettuce.

"*Pa que seas lechuguero y ganes muchos dólares[116],*" he used to tell him.

It was very physical and demanding work but it yielded much more money than other kinds of field work. My father refused at first, but later he followed my uncle's advice. He began to learn the trade of *los lechugueros.* My father's transition to the lettuce industry opened more possibilities for our family. My father was hired by Joe Maggio. The company had work in Imperial Valley and in King City. Both my parents could work all year since Joe Maggio grew a variety of crops. The best part of all was that the company provided adequate housing in King City. We were so happy; at last we would live in the company's beautiful camp during the summer. This series of events gave our family more stability. For three years we had been moving to many different places in search of work. The constant change of schools was very hard on the children. We were always the new kids in strange and sometimes hostile environments. Now we would be in only two schools during the year. We could make friends and keep them. My father worked in the lettuce while my mother worked harvesting other crops with the same company. My sister Silvia and I were able to work during holidays and the summer time to help increase the family income.

"*ésta ser tu cabina[117],*" said *el campero.*

He showed us our cabin. We went in and explored the interior. It was the largest we had lived in since our arrival a few years back. It had two bedrooms, a kitchen, and a large area that served as living room

---

[116] So you become a lettuce harvester and earn many dollars.

[117] This is your cabin

dining room combination. Most important of all, it had an indoor, full bathroom, with shower and sink. We felt like royalty. The camp had the best housing available in the area. It was the best we'd had. The first days were boring since we were the first family to arrive. Most of the residents were *sanahorieros*[118] and their season started a few weeks later. There were only a few *desahijadores* who worked *en el cortito* thinning lettuce. It was the first stage in the process of growing lettuce.

"*Los zanahorieros llegaron*[119]," shouted my mother through the window.

We all ran out and saw a caravan formed by five station wagons and two cars. They were loaded with luggage, cardboard boxes and items hanging from racks and half open trunks. There was a blue, old model station wagon with a smiling child with orange hair looking out the rolled down window.

"He looks like a carrot," said my sister. The similarity was amazing.

"Maybe it is because he ate too many carrots," said my sister smiling. "He looks cute," she added, as she followed the vehicle with her eyes until it stopped a few cabins away from ours.

It was a large family. We walked close to see them unpack their belongings. Everybody helped. We saw a girl and a boy about our age, teenagers, and two smaller ones, less than ten years of age. It was great news for us. After a few weeks without having friends in the camp we longed for someone to spend the gusty King City afternoons with.

My sisters, brother and I were used to being lonesome for prolonged periods of time. We had learned to get along and play together. In times of solitude we enjoyed reading. My sister Silvia and I became avid readers. We devoured novels at two or three a week; we were addicted. We were usually the best readers in school. We read both English and

---

[118] Carrot harvesters

[119] The carrot harvesters arrived

Spanish books. I liked everything: fiction, biographies, history, comics, adventures and love stories. My sister also liked most of the books I read and we usually shared them. One of our favorite activities was to visit the library. We could check out up to three books. But it was great to have friends to spend time with. We were teenagers and our interests also included hanging around, listening to music and talking. Now, with all these new families arriving we would have friends our age.

We made several friends in the new camp. We spent time together in school and in the afternoons we hung around a laundry. We usually listened to music inside the laundry room, which served as refuge from the gusty winds. My sister made friends with a girl named Maria Elena. She was Juanito's sister, the boy with orange hair. I did not like her. She was the most beautiful girl in school but I despised her flirtatious behavior. She dressed in very short skirts, showing her skinny legs. She walked with an extreme swing of her hips getting the attention of all the boys in school. I felt she was provoking all the boys with her beauty and her extravagant outfits. I had constant fights with my sister when I saw them together.

"I don't like her as your friend. Don't bring her to our house. She is not good for you *mensa*[120]," I would tell Silvia.

She always answered angrily with insults.

"*Tu no me vas a decir con quien me junte pendejo*[121]," she yelled at me.

Maria Elena was always nice to me. She smiled, but I never smiled back. Yet, I always presented a mean expression hoping she would feel my rejection. I wanted her to know I didn't like her and I wanted her out of my view. I always watched her walk until she disappeared from my sight. I could not understand why I always spied on her after she left. My sister noticed how I looked at Maria Elena and she teased me.

"Doesn't she look neat in that outfit?" Silvia would ask.

I tried to ignore Silvia and dismissed anything she said about her. When Maria Elena approached me I always rejected her. But when I saw her talking with other boys I became angry. I hated her even more for always showing off.

Cruising was very popular in King City. Teenagers who had access to a car would spend hours driving up and down Broadway Street. They would drive very slowly with their radios or eight tracks playing at full blast. Most of the Anglo kids cruising would drive in nice sport cars. They had Thunderbirds, Firebirds and Camaros. Mexican teens were lucky to drive the family station wagon. Some of the older ones, who worked, saved enough money to buy older Chevys and Fords. One of my friends, Fidencio, had a 1963 Impala. I usually cruised with him and other friends. When Fidencio was not around, I would ask my father to use our station wagon. Silvia and I liked to cruise when my father allowed me to use the family car. We would buy a bag of cherries and toured Broadway listening to *Los Freddy's, Little Joe y Los Relampagos del*

---

[120] Silly.

[121] You are not going to tell me who to hang around with, stupid.

81

Norte[122].

It was common and convenient for farm worker families to teach their children to drive at very young age. I learned to drive at age twelve. I sat on a pillow to look taller and wore a hat to look older. At first I only drove on dirt roads around the fields. My father would send me to move the car to keep it close to us during the day. We had our ice chest with cold water, drinks, and our food. Soon, I learned to drive on city streets. I could take my mother to the laundry or run errands to the store. Later I began driving on highways. It was most practical for my father; without the worry to drive home, he would usually get drunk when we visited friends. In one occasion, we went to the Imperial Valley to visit family and tend to some business over the weekend. My father got drunk and was not able to drive back. My mother was furious; she worried missing work the next day.

"*Por culpa de tu pinchi vicio vamos a perder de trabajar[123],*" she told my father angrily.

My father mumbled a few incomprehensible phrases and continued sleeping and snoring as loudly as an angry lion.

"*No te preocupes[124]*, I will drive mother," I said, trying to console her and playing the role of the responsible male of the family.

My mother trusted my driving more than my father's when he was intoxicated. I had experienced driving on highways many times, but I had never driven through Los Angeles; it was a great challenge that I eagerly took. We loaded my father in the cargo area, where he continued sleeping throughout the trip. We secured the younger children in the back seat and proceeded with the 550 mile journey. The trip was exciting. It was tense when I was in heavy traffic in Los Angeles, but it

---

[122] Popular Hispanic musical groups of the 70's.

[123] Because of your damn bad habit we will miss work.

[124] Don't worry

gave me a great feeling of accomplishment. I was thrilled when I was able to overtake many cars when my mother was not looking at the speedometer. When she sensed we were going too fast, she would urge me to slow down. I was relieved when we reached our destination. I was able to help my mother and I had earned the right to borrow the car when I had the need.

"¿Qué *onda guey, vas a ir al baile*[125]?" Fidencio asked me.

He had parked his car by the grassy area next to my house and jumped out excited about our plans to attend the dance. The weekly dance was the best entertainment in King City. The city's fairgrounds were famous throughout the valley for its dances. Many Mexican and Texan groups played to entertain the exhausted workers. This week was going to be one of the most exiting events: *Los Relámpagos Del Norte*[126] was going to perform. They were one of the most popular groups and the dance promised to be great. It was advertised one hundred miles around the valley. Everyone we knew had plans to attend.

"*Simon*[127], I wouldn't miss it for anything in the world," I answered with enthusiasm.

"We need to get to the fairgrounds early so my father can let us in for free," said Fidencio, proud about his connection at the event.

Fidencio's father tended the concession stand and had access to the dance hall.

"We need to wait for Eraclio," I answered. "He should be here soon."

Eraclio was one of our friends who worked with us during the summer harvesting bell pepper. He was older than us and did not go to

---

[125] Idiomatic slang (What is happening ox, are you going to the dance?)

[126] A popular music group.

[127] An affirmative expression (Yes).

school. He had dropped out and worked full time.

"Is he coming?" asked Fidencio. "Did he get the beer?"

"Yes," I said. "His brother bought a case of Coors for us. He will be here soon. Let's wait for him."

Eraclio had a large family. He had older brothers and sisters and he was allowed to drink. They would buy beer for us to get high before the dance every week.

"We can drink the beer at my house. No one is home," said Fidencio. "But we need to hurry before the sponsors of the dance get to the fairgrounds. If we delay, we will have to pay admission. This week they will charge ten dollars."

We saw Eraclio coming and urged him to hurry.

"*Apurate guey*[128]," Fidencio and I shouted.

After drinking a few beers we headed for the dance. We left some drinks in the car for later in the night.

From inside the concession stand we saw how people started to pour in the dance hall. Every one was wearing their best garments. The men came to the dance wearing their Levis, colorful shirts with square designs and hats trying to look as *Norteño*[129] or Texan as possible. The women looked sexy, wearing excessive makeup and mini-skirts. The single girls smiled, flirting with the men as they came in, while the married ones acted serious trying not to attract attention from other men to avoid a jealous outburst from their husbands. Many married men went alone with intentions of scoring with other women while their wives stayed at home caring for their children. Everyone pretended to be happy; they left their problems at home and tried to enjoy themselves for a few hours. The men acted courteous with the women in their intent to impress them and not let their *machismo* or manly manners transpire, ruining their

---

[128] Idiomatic slang (Hurry up ox).

[129] From the north.

opportunity to get acquainted with the girls. The women would resist this kind of behavior by refusing to dance. On the other hand, they were compliant with men who treated them with respect. The dance empowered the women, who were otherwise abused and control by the men in their lives: fathers, boyfriends, husbands, and bosses.

Just then, a group of beautiful girls passed in front of us flirting, as if inviting us to dance.

"*Mira ése ramillete de flores*[130]," said Eraclio, referring to the beautiful girls. "I think they want me to dance with them," he insisted.

"Good luck," said Fidencio, laughing. "Use something to cover your nose," he laughed again.

Fidencio knew the girls worked at the Basic, a factory that processed garlic and onions. Everyone that worked there was penetrated by the strong odor of the garlic. You could smell the stench from a distance and it became uncomfortable with proximity. The odor was a nuisance and it tarnished the beauty of the girls.

The floor was full of couples dancing and having a good time. Most couples danced Texan style, circling the dancing floor with a variety of dance steps. Some danced to get attention with their agile moves. Others danced close together, getting intimate as they hugged and kissed, displaying their attraction towards each other. Fidencio and Eraclio both had girlfriends and were waiting for them to dance. When their girls arrived they would be dancing cheek to cheek, softly talking and kissing. I was not as lucky, so I had to wait for girls that I knew to be available. It was a competition to get dancing partners. Many men were after a few girls and they had the luxury to choose their dancing partners. I did not like to be rejected so I was careful in asking only girls I knew would accept dancing with me. I knew some girls from the

---

[130] Look at that flower bouquet.

camp and from school. I also knew some girls from work, but they were difficult to identify. At work, they covered their faces with handkerchiefs and wore sunglasses and big hats which covered their faces. It was hard to recognize them in the glamorous attire they wore for the dance.

The dance was a great success. As always it served its purpose: the people were alleviated from their troubles for a few hours. The next day it was back to their regular routines. Working in the fields was hard on everyone but more for women. They worked just as hard as men but were paid less just for being women. Men would go home and rest or have a few beers with their friends at Nina's Cantina, a popular bar on Broadway Street. The women had to continue with the house chores, cleaning the house, washing the clothes, and preparing the food. I hated to see my mother work so hard only to return home and continue with house chores while my father got drunk with his friends.

Women also suffered from many more injustices while working in the fields. They were discriminated against and abused. Going to the restroom was always difficult for women. Men could just move to the side, inside a canal or behind a bush. Women needed more privacy but the most they had was a portable bathroom which was often filthy because of the lack of cleaning or due to spillage when it was being transported through the bumpy roads. Women had to endure listening to abusive language from the men. It was common for foremen to impose on single and some married women. They were victims of sexual harassment, sexual favors in exchange for job security. Some abusive foremen took advantage of the illegal status of some women who could not reject sexual advances in fear of being reported to emigration and facing deportation.

During the summer I worked harvesting bell pepper. It was a large crew of over one hundred workers, of which only twenty were legal residents. The rest were illegal. When the immigration officers came to check our documents, they would flee or be arrested. The crew would be severely dismantled for a few days until the workers returned or the foreman would hire other illegal workers. Those of us who were legal received preferential treatment because we were the few reliable workers who would continue with the harvest when the raids took place. I was part of a six men crew of loaders. Fidencio and Eraclio were also part of the crew. The other members were *el Chato, el Indio*[131] and Javier. The harvesters would fill buckets with bell peppers and we would load them on trailers.

"Hey! Lucio, move the car to this end of the field," shouted Fidencio. "It is almost break time and I have some *tacos* in my lunch box."

We were getting near the end of the field and his car was at the opposite side. I ran to the car which was next to the bus that transported the rest of the crew. As I approached the bus I heard a moan, then a female voice pleading with someone to leave her alone.

"*No por favor*[132]," said the female.

Then I heard a male voice.

"*No te va a pasar nada si no resistes*[133]," said the man in a threatening voice.

I recognized the man's voice. It was the foreman, *el Sopilote*[134]. That was his nickname. For short they called him *Sopi*. Based on the noises and exchanged of words, I assumed he was trying to force himself on one of the illegal girls. He had been courting a lady and her three young daughters. He hired them knowing they were illegal and his intentions were to seduce them. He isolated the young girls from the rest of the

---

[131] Nick names: Flat nose and Indian

[132] No, please.

[133] Nothing will happen to you, if you don't resist?

[134] The vulture

crew by giving them the task of cleaning the bus. Later, when the crew was far away, he would go in there and molest them. According to the rumors, he had seduced the mother and two older daughters. He was after his younger pray, Carmen, who was only fifteen years old. I was disgusted to witness this aggression. I knew there was little I could do. The family had been threatened by *el Sopi*. They were afraid to be reported to immigration and be deported. I intentionally made a loud noise that startled *Sopi*. Scared by the noise, he allowed the girl to go. Sopi did not want witnesses of his actions. The young girl ran away crying. I stayed there until she was far away from the bus, far from the grasp of *el Sopi*.

I drove the car to where the crew was taking the morning break. I was mad, but glad I had stopped the foreman's action.

"*Agarre al pinchi Sopi* [135]trying to rape the younger of the new girls," I told my friends. "He sent her to clean the bus and then he sneaked on her."

"*Pinchi Sopilote*, he saw me talking to Carmen and he threatened to fire me if I spoke to her again," said *el Indio*. "He wants all the girls for himself."

"*Nomás las mojadas*[136]," said Fidencio annoyed by the incident. "*Pinchi, joto*[137], he is taking advantage of them."

Sopi approached the crew. He was upset, and walked nervously across the rows, pretending to inspect the baskets full of bell peppers and the rows of plants already harvested. He went near Carmen and her mother several times, stopping and staring in an intimidating way. He suddenly stopped a few meters away from us facing the crew

---

[135] I caught damn Sopi

[136] Only wetbacks

[137] Damn fag

and his back toward us. He stood with his arms crossed, lost deep in his thoughts. We looked at each other and silently smiled. Fidencio grabbed a large firm bell pepper. He showed it to us and made a throwing motion towards *Sopi*. We looked at each other and nodded, understanding the prank. We each picked the hardest bell pepper we could find. We took aim, and threw the bell peppers as hard as we could; aiming at Sopi's head. The bell peppers smashed on Sopi's head and back, stunning him. He dropped to the ground covering his head, confused by the sudden impacts on his body. He stood up angrily when he identified the projectiles as harmless and figured out where they came from. *Sopi* got on his feet and approached us furiously.

"*Hijos de su*[138] *#@%*," shouted *el Sopi*, directing his rage at us.

He knew the peppers came from our direction, but he did not know who threw them.

"*Me la van a pagar hijos de su #@%*[139]," he repeated again.

Suddenly he stopped and started laughing like a maniac.

"You are jealous," *Sopi* said with immense joy. "You are mad because all the girls in this crew are mine."

He roared with laughter. He jumped up and down like a crazed man.

"They are mine, you hear! *Son mías aunque les arda*[140]." Sopi barked at us.

He was enjoying his moment of supremacy. He looked at us defiantly. Then he turned around and left laughing and mumbling insults toward us.

---

[138] Sons of a

[139] You will pay for this (#@%) strong insults.

[140] They are mine even if it bugs you.

"*Se encabrono[141],*" said el Indio, smiling and enjoying the outcome of our prank.

"*Va hacienda chile con el yo –yo[142],*" Fidencio added sarcastically.

"He is going to fire us," said el Chato, concerned about the reaction of el Sopi. "He is vindictive. He will black ball us with every employer in the valley."

"*Que se meta el jale por el yo-yo[143],*" I said. "Let's not worry about losing our work. He needs us; we are the only loaders with legal papers in the crew. He will not risk losing us. Besides, I don't think I want to work here any more. I can't stand witnessing all this exploitation."

Sopi did not approach us for the rest of the day. He isolated himself from the rest of the crew leaving the supervision to his assistants. He looked at the crew from far away. He appeared to be thinking, perhaps planning his revenge against our mutiny.

At the end of the day, the harvesters were transported in the bus back to their homes. We always stayed for at least an hour loading the bell peppers and then went home in our own car. *Sopi* was waiting for us at the end of the field next to Fidencio's car.

"No hard feelings," he said cynically, as we approached him. "I deserve the prank." He let go a long, loud laugh.

"Listen," said *Sopi*. "You need the work and I need good loaders. Let's make a deal. You get off my affairs and I will forget the incident."

He laughed again. Then his expression turned menacing.

"But if you continue to interfere, I will get you. You know I can," he threatened us.

Sopi turned around, walked to his truck and drove off. We looked at

---

[141] He got mad

[142] He is making hot sauce with his butt. Idiomatic expression that means he is throwing a big tantrum.

[143] He can take his job and shove it.

each other confused as to what to do next.

"I don't know about you, but I am going to look for work in another place," I told my friends.

We all agreed to protest by not showing up the next day. We decided to search for work in another crew. The harvest was at its peak and there were plenty of places to find work.

Fidencio dropped me off at my house after work. My father confronted me as I open the front door. He demanded an explanation for my behavior with el *Sopilote*. Apparently the news about the incident traveled fast; my father knew about it before I reached home.

"¿*Que chingados paso*[144]?" my father barked at me. "*El Sopi* is a good friend. He does us many favors when we work with him. Why do you have to interfere in his affairs?" he demanded loudly.

My father continued with a long sermon that I tried to ignore. He provoked me with his insults and demanded I go and apologize to *El Sopi*. I made it clear that I would not apologize. I tried to explain but he would not reason with me.

"We only hit him with bell peppers. He did not get hurt," I said.

My mother advocated in my favor. She put herself between my father and me, concerned my father would smack me. He was a big man and turned violent when mad.

"*Le hubieran mochado los huevos al cabrón*[145]," my mother said reproaching the abuse by *El Sopi*.

My mother cautioned my father against any aggression towards me. "*Déjalo en paz*," [146]she defended me, valiantly.

She was tired of hearing his insults and his threats every time he got drunk. She was not about to let him harass her children anymore.

---

[144] What the hell happened?

[145] They should have cut his damn balls.

[146] Leave him alone.

I did not want the confrontation to escalate; I left the house until things calmed down.

"*Esta loco*[147]. Apologize to that *cerdo*[148]. I'd rather die," I mumbled to myself.

Besides, I had already decided not to work for *El Sopi* anymore. Eraclio had an uncle that was a foreman and he needed workers. I would work with him the rest of the summer. I walked down the street in the cold windy afternoon waiting for my father to leave the house. It always happened this way. He would provoke a conflict then use it as an excuse to go to the local bar to continue drinking.

---

[147] He is crazy

[148] Pig

LOS CHAVISTAS

"*¿Quieres ir a Salinas*[149]?" asked my mother.

"*Sí. ¿Quieres que vaya*[150]?" I said smiling.

It was always exciting to go to Salinas on the weekends. It was nice to get away from the monotony of King City. Salinas is a large city and there were many things to do. We usually went shopping at Monte Mart, a large department store. Monte Mart was well stocked. You could find food, clothes, appliances, electronics, and many other items. *El Burrito* [151]was another store we liked to visit. It was a small grocery store that sold mostly Mexican items: tortillas, spices, magazines, and other miscellaneous items popular among farm workers. There was also a large park where we went to eat Kentucky Fried Chicken and attend a variety of activities that took place during the weekends. There were musical groups that played free for the public. On occasion, we could see dancers, small traveling circuses, or fairs. This week there was a large rally for farm workers. A popular activist, César Chávez, was going to speak to gather support for the United Farm Workers of America, a

---

[149] Do you want to go to Salinas?

[150] Yes. Do you want me to go?

[151] Little donkey

union trying to organize farm labor. My mother and father talked about it during the 50 mile drive from King City. They said that the farm workers were tired of the treatment from the farmers and employers. The workers argued that they were being exploited and abused and that they needed protection from the union to gain respect, better wages, and appropriate benefits. Hundreds of people attended the assembly. Many went to support the cause; others were just curious.

There were many who were intimidated by the coming events. A possible strike meant missing work or facing potential hardship. There were many accounts of violent incidents between the *Chavistas*[152], the employers, and their followers. Both sides accused each other of starting the confrontations. The Chavistas formed their picket lines in strategic places where they could block the entrance of the strike breakers into the fields to work. The scabs tried to force their way into the fields, while the strikers put up a strong resistance. The confrontations included verbal confrontations and fist fights. On some occasions, things got out of hand and rocks were thrown, shattering vehicle windows and injuring people from both sides. The employers hired armed body guards to protect the scabs and intimidate the strikers. The guards would patrol the edge of the fields with ferocious dogs and showed their guns to the strikers in an attempt to scare them away. The Chavistas were not intimidated. Instead, they saw the show of power as a provocation to escalate the violence. The union leaders always preached non-violence. They would say in their speeches that violence would not benefit the union. The leaders encouraged their followers to control their emotions and not become part of violent incidents. It was important to keep a peaceful image and reputation to gain the support of powerful politicians and the general population.

---

[152] Chavez Followers

On one side of the park was a large stage. Several speakers would get on the platform and give supportive speeches. We tried to get as near to the stage as possible to listen. There was a great excitement among the crowd. Their leader, César Chávez, would make a speech to officially start the Salinas Campaign. The union had a very successful campaign in central California. Large grape growing companies had signed important contracts with the union and its workers. These contracts provided the union members with medical benefits, paid vacation time, a good salary and most importantly, respect for the workers. It was a great victory; the union had gained respect and acceptance. They wanted to spread the success to other areas, and Salinas was the most important area at that stage of the growing season. The last thing the union wanted was violent incidents that would tarnish the peaceful image they had displayed up until that point.

Cesar Chávez climbed the stage to make his speech amongst a loud ovation from his followers. Everyone cheered in excitement.

"*¡Viva Chávez*[153]*!*" the crowd shouted at the top of their lungs.

"*¡Viva la huelga! ¡Vivan los campesinos*[154]*!*" the chavistas insisted.

The excitement was contagious; even I was chanting the song *De Colores*[155] with the multitude. *Cesar Chavez* spoke about the confrontation with the farmers. He said it was essential to support the movement until the end. He spoke of boycotting products of the largest company, Sun Harvest, to pressure the lettuce industry to sign a decent contract. The people responded by chanting *¡Viva Chávez! ¡Viva la huelga! ¡Vivan los campesinos! ¡Abajo con los rancheros*[156]*! ¡Viva la causa*[157]*!* The leader

---

[153] Long live Chavez!

[154] Long live the strike! Long live the farm workers!

[155] Of colors.

[156] Down with the farmers!

[157] Long live the cause.

explained the benefits of a good contract. He said that contracts would bring stability and prosperity to the workplace and that it would help the farm worker's children get a good education. The people loved to hear Cesar Chávez speak. He brought hope for the desperate situation of many farm workers. He encouraged the people to speak up and fight for their rights. He encouraged parents to send their children to school in quest of a better future through education. Cesar Chávez did not have fear of the powerful farmers. He was a great role model and he gave moral and emotional strength to the farm workers who had worked under intimidating conditions for many years. At the end of the rally the crowed left inspired and enthusiastic about *la causa*. They were ready to strike if necessary to get a good contract.

"*¡Mira, un chingo de carros*[158]*!* Said Fidencio, impressed by the huge caravan of cars approaching the fields we were working.

"*Son los Chavistas*," I exclaimed, amazed at the spectacle.

Every car carried workers waving flags. The flags had the union colors and emblem; red with a black circle in the center, and in it a white eagle.

Hundreds of *Chavistas*, surrounded the field. The strike had begun. The *Chavistas* got off the cars and began approaching the edge of the field, carrying flags and posters and shouting "*¡Viva la huelga!*" "*¡Únanse a la causa compañeros*[159]*!*" A man with a portable speaker asked the people to stop working and join the caravan in a demonstration of solidarity. He said that we needed to strike to force the employers to negotiate a good contract. The whole crew stopped the labor and walked off the field to join the crowd. Not all workers were sympathetic to *la causa*. They mumbled their disapproval amongst themselves, but complied with the request, intimidated by the circumstances. The majority wanted the

---

[158] Look, so many cars. (Chingo) is an idiomatic expression that means (many)

[159] Join the cause companions!

strike to begin. Many people thought that it would end soon. They did not perceive that it could become a difficult conflict and that the strikers would have to endure sacrifices to survive the struggle. We followed the caravan to a large, isolated area where other caravans were meeting. There was stage set up to hold an informational meeting. One of the high officials of César Chávez informed everyone about the present events. He said the strike had begun that morning and that it would continue until the farmers signed a contract. There was no going back, and all farm workers needed to support *la causa* to defeat the powerful farmers. The speaker also gave information about the union benefits that would be provided for the people who helped in the picket lines. Each family member who participated in the strike would receive a ration of gasoline, a food dispense or voucher, and ninety dollars a week. Everyone was very confident that victory would be certain and swift.

My family, just like most people, at first joined the cause. Every one wanted a contract. But many workers joined just because they were intimidated by the multitude supporting *la causa*. They did not want to have a confrontation with *los Chavistas*. We participated in the picket lines everyday for two weeks. There was plenty of action during the mornings when *los esquiroles*[160] were transported into the fields to work, breaking the picket line. We tried to stop them by placing barriers such as cars, tree stumps, or other bulky items. There were some occasions when people made human barriers, only to be moved away by the police who were very alert to prevent any violence. Some *Chavistas*, who got emotional and put up a strong resistance, were beaten with batons and arrested by the police. During the day we kept vigil over the fields where *esquiroles* where working. When the *esquiroles* were near the edge of the field, we would try to talk to them to stop laboring and join *la causa*.

---

[160] The scabs (people who break the strike by crossing the picket line to work)

Some *Chavistas* lost control of their emotions and shouted obscenities at the scabs. But the scabs were safe behind the police lines. They also had the protection of the hired, armed bodyguards with dogs, who patrolled the outskirts of the fields. At the end of the day, the confrontations were more intense. *Los Chavistas*, frustrated by the scabbing, escalated the insults and threw rocks at the vehicles that transported the *esquiroles*. As the strike progressed, the violent incidents increased and people began to get discouraged. It was obvious that the strike would not end as swiftly as it was first perceived.

My parents became concerned for our safety. They were being pressured to work, or to abandon the house where we lived. The house was provided by the company and they would not house anyone involved with the *Chavistas*. I heard them talking about taking the children to Imperial Valley and returning to work. The companies were paying exaggerated salaries to encourage the people to take the risk of scabbing. My father felt badly about crossing the picket lines, but our savings were disappearing fast. We could not afford to continue the strike. My father received a great offer by a friend to work harvesting lettuce. Housing and meals were free and the pay was more than triple the original wages. Many people had abandoned the picket lines and went back to work, persuaded by the offers of the employers. *Los esquiroles* were persecuted by the *Chavistas*. The peaceful *causa* became violent and the farm workers began to fight among themselves.

We left my brother and sisters in the Imperial Valley, and my father, mother and I returned to King City to work harvesting lettuce. We did not want to break the strike but we needed to work. We felt bad about going against *la causa*, but picketing was a great sacrifice that my father was not about to take any longer. On the other hand, we would be working for enormous wages enabling us to make up what we had lost during the weeks we had been on strike. We would stay for a month until work began in Imperial Valley. The earnings were good but it was dangerous to cross the picket line. In the mornings we would sneak into the parking lot of the company's shed. We would board a bus with windows covered with plywood to protect us from projectiles thrown by the *Chavistas* as we entered the fields. We would work daily from sunrise to sunset and return to our quarters only to sleep and rest for the next day. We kept a low profile to prevent unwanted encounters with the *Chavistas*.

It was my first opportunity to be hired as a *lechugero*. There was such a large demand for laborers that they were hiring children and old people who did not even know how to cut and pack lettuce. The company had people training the new workers to cut the lettuce and pay them by the hour. The packers were paid by piece work at the rate of one dollar per box.

"*Este es el Wino*[161]," said the foreman, introducing a drunken man to me and another teenager named Jose.

"*Órale vatos, si trabajan duro, les pago veinticinco centavos la caja*[162]," el Wino said to us.

We agreed. We would get our hourly wages, plus Jose and I would share twenty five-cents for each box el Wino packed. He could pack three hundred boxes per day, doubling our daily earnings. El *Wino* knew that if he was to make money he needed fast workers. To encourage us to cut fast, he offered us part of his earnings. El *Wino* taught us how to cut faster and to pack boxes. It was convenient for him but more for us. Besides earning more money, we were learning the trades of a *lechuguero*; both Jose and I wanted to be *lechugueros* some day. I worked for two weeks. My father took me to Imperial Valley when school started and he and my mother returned to King City to work for a few more days.

---

[161] This is Wino (Wine drinker)

[162] OK guys, if you work hard, I will pay you twenty five cents a box.

EL CAMPEÓN

RETURNING TO SCHOOL IN Calexico was a relief after the turbulent summer in King City. It was also exciting since it was my first year in junior high school. My mother enrolled me at De Anza Junior High School as a seventh grader. For the first time, I experienced having multiple teachers and physical education. The first day was chaotic; I was shy about dressing and gave some bullies a reason to tease and harass me. As we were playing basket ball, a tall eighth grader named McNish insisted with his teasing game. He got upset because he could not keep me from scoring. I was too fast for McNish. I played my best to impress the coach, Mr. Belcher, and the other students. I took the ball away from McNish and scored. He was upset and pounded the ball on the ground.

"You fouled me!" he said angrily.

I smiled happily to myself for teaching the bully a lesson in basketball. McNish dribbled towards me again and tried to pass me to score. Again, I took the ball away from him and scored. McNish threw the ball at me. I blocked it with my knee and the ball bounced back, hitting McNish in the face. He became furious and approached me, calling me names and insulting. I stood my ground quietly. He pushed me and slapped me in the face. Before the coach intervened, I clinched my fist and responded with a hard punch, knocking McNished to the ground. He fell down hard and hit his head on the ground. Mr. Belcher held me down while another coach went to check on McNish. The bully felt lightheaded by the punch and the surprise of my reaction. He was used to pushing students around and did not expect a small seventh grader to knock him on his butt. Mr. Belcher took me to the office followed by the other coach escorting McNish. They took us to our principal Mr. Porter's office.

"You are the new student?" Mr. Porter asked. "You just registered today, didn't you?" he added.

I nodded my headed, looking down to the ground.

"Are you going to be like this all the time?" the principal asked.

"No," I responded. "I was just defending myself. He hit me for no reason," I added.

Mr. Porter looked at McNish and in an angry tone he asked, "What happened? You found your match, Mr. McNish? This little fellow knocked you down? I am amazed," he said.

Apparently McNish had a bad reputation with the principal. He was notorious for being a bully and had been in the office many times for harassing other students.

"OK, I'll tell you what I will do," said Mr. Porter. "I will give you one paddle for fighting, Lucio. I will give you three paddles for harassing a smaller student, Mr. McNish."

The principal proceeded to get his paddle. It was large, with a handle made to fit his hand, giving him a good grip. The paddle had several rows of small holes. Mr. Porter bragged that it was a paddle with air dynamics. The principal ordered McNish out of the office. When he went out, Mr. Porter asked me to take everything out off my back pockets and to bend over. I bent over and put my hands on my knees for support. I closed my eyes and waited for the paddle to strike my butt. I felt the hard spank and a sting ran up and down my body. I almost cried out from the pain but I contained myself.

"I hope I don't see you in my office any more, sir," Mr. Porter warned me.

I left the office still hurting from the spanking. McNish went in after me to receive his punishment. I returned to class. Mr. Belcher told me to join a group that was running laps. I caught up with them and ran four laps and went to the showers. PE was the last class of the day so we did not have to hurry in the showers. I waited at my locker for the other students to leave. Mr. Belcher approached me and asked, "Why are you not showering?"

"I am waiting for the others to finish," I said.

"I saw you running. You're a good runner. Would you like to join the cross country team?" Mr. Belcher asked me.

We talked for a while, exchanging information. He told me about the races. I told him about myself. From the first time I met Mr. Belcher, a friendship began to develop. He was a good coach and person and inspired me with trust. I joined the cross country team and did very well. Later in the year, I also joined wrestling and track. I had a hard time going to the races and tournaments since they took place mostly on Saturdays. I was always working in the field on Saturdays. My father would take me and would not allow me to miss work to participate in sports. During an open house, Mr. Belcher talked to my father about letting me go to the sport events. My father insisted that I had to work.

"We are poor," my father said. "Everyone needs to help."

My mother intervened, supporting me. She asked my father to let me go to some of the events, but my father rejected her proposal. I did not want this incident to create a problem for my mother. She had enough fights with my father because of his drinking problem. I didn't want to give my father another reason for him to harass my mother. I stopped going to practice and gave up the idea of participating in sports.

A few days later, Mr. Belcher called me to his office after school.

"What happened? Why are you missing practice?" he asked. "Are you sick?" he insisted.

"No, I quit the team," I responded sadly. "My father won't let me go to the races. There is no sense in practicing."

"I will talk to your father again," Mr. Belcher said.

"No, he won't let me go. We need the money. I need to help my family," I tried to explain.

"How much do you earn on Saturdays?" Mr. Belcher asked.

"Sixteen dollars a day," I answered.

"What if I hired you and paid you that money? Would your father let you go?" Mr. Belcher asked.

"Would you do that for me?" I asked incredulous. "That would be great," I said.

Mr. Belcher laughed at my excitement. I really enjoyed representing my school in competitions. I had developed into a diverse athlete and could compete at a good level in all school sports. I ran home to tell my mother the good news. She was so happy to see my smile. My mother knew that sports were important for me and she sensed my disappointment when my father denied me the opportunity to play. She was very supportive and offered to talk to my father about Mr. Belcher's offer. She was concerned that his negative reaction would upset me and I would revolt against him. I had confronted him before when he harassed my mother. I would get between them when they were fighting and I would threaten him not to touch her. They had constant fights because my father would go and spend his check drinking with his friends. Later, he expected to cover the living costs with my mother's check. When he returned from drinking, my father was always violent against us. My brother, my sisters, and I were used to the scuffles. We would always side with my mother and wrestled him away from her when he tried to hurt her. The next day he would wake up complaining about his hangover and beg my mother for forgiveness. She always gave in to his pleads. We would have peace for a few days and then the cycle would repeat again. My mother went and talked to my father, who was drinking beer and watching a soccer game. She tried to explain that I could work for sixteen dollars on Sunday to make up for missing a day in the fields.

"*Así Lucio puede jugar el sábado[163],*" my mother said softly, imploring all the saints for my father's approval. "*El profesor le va pagar[164],*" she explained.

My father looked at her for a few seconds than started laughing.

"*Que bueno que le pague, así trae doble el dinero: dieciséis el sábado y dieciséis el domingo[165],*" he said sarcastically.

He laughed for a long time about his joke.

"*¿Esta chistoso, verdad[166]?*" he asked.

I did not hear what they said after that. I left the house, disappointed. I had hoped that with Mr. Belcher's offer I would be able to play. I walked around the block to cool off. I later returned home and sneaked in through the window to avoid facing my father. I was disgusted. I went to bed immediately. As I tried to burrow inside my blankets, I felt my mother's hand caressing my hair.

"*Dijo que estaba bien[167],*" she said softly.

I turned around in disbelief. She smiled at me as she cuddled me and reassured me that I would play regardless of what my father said. I don't know what she said to him, but it was the first time I saw her stand

---

[163] That way Lucio can play on Saturday.

[164] The teacher will pay him.

[165] It is good that he pays him, that way he brings double the money, sixteen on Saturday and sixteen on Sunday.

[166] Its funny, isn't it?

[167] He said it was OK.

up to him and act against his will. I promised my mother I would do my best in school and sports.

My best school experience was at De Anza during seventh and eighth grade. As a seventh grader, I went through a very rewarding adaptation period. I did well both in sports and academics. I participated in cross country, wrestling, and track and field. In academics my performance was average but it culminated by my making the honor roll in the last semester. My mother, and eventually my father, was very happy about my accomplishments. During eighth grade is when I excelled in school. It was the only year that I attended only one school for the entire year. My parents could not come to the Imperial Valley when school started. They had to complete the harvest cycle in King City and work in Imperial Valley would start one month after. I would be graduating to the high school at the end of the year, and I wanted to do it in style. I persuaded my parents to allow me to live by myself in the house we rented in Calexico to enable me to start school. I was only fourteen and my mother was concerned for my well being.

"¿Quién *te va a dar de comer*[168]? She asked.

"*No te preocupes Madre*[169]," I reassured her with a smile.

"*Déjalo, ya esta grande*[170]," said my father, proud that I would take the challenge of caring for myself. "*No te podemos dar mucho dinero*[171]," he said, and advised me to use the money wisely.

I insisted that I would be fine. I could take care of my basic needs at home and as far as money was concerned, I knew a few foremen that could hire me to work on weekends. In two days I could make more than enough money to meet my needs.

---

[168] Who will feed you?

[169] Don't worry mother.

[170] Let him, he is grown up.

[171] We cannot give a lot of money.

We had a very happy reunion when they returned a month later. My parents were proud that I had managed to thrive on my own for such a long time.

"*Me dio mucho pendiente, pero me da gusto que todo salió bién*[172]," said my mother relieved.

During this period of time, I managed to achieve many goals. I was able to attend football, summer camp, and I made the school's team. I played starting quarterback and finished the season as the most valuable player. Attending the games wasn't a problem because we played during school days in the afternoon. It didn't interfere with my responsibility of working on the weekends to help the family. Mr. Belcher was our coach. We had become very good friends and he continued to advise me and always offered his support. I always gave my best effort in his Physical Education class and the team. During the cross country and wrestling seasons there were several weekend events that caused me to miss work on Saturdays. Mr. Belcher continued to hire me to do chores at his house and he paid me to make up for the lost wages. I usually worked doing odd jobs in the afternoon and on Sundays. I also participated in the cross country team as one of the top seven members of the team. I was a good long distance runner. I was not the best in the team but I contributed to winning the county championship.

The sport where I excelled the most was wrestling. I was a novice and I had learned only a few basic techniques, but my ability was well refined. I was quick, clever, and I could execute the few defensive and offensive moves on almost anyone that wrestled me. I had an impenetrable defensive stand that could disable most attacks. My offensive arsenal was small but a couple of my attacks were unstoppable. I was undefeated in Imperial Valley in the one hundred and twenty pound category and

---

[172] I was worried, but I am glad everything came out right.

qualified for the state Junior Olympics Wrestling Championships held in San Diego, California. I was elated about the trip; I had never been to San Diego before. I had heard many conversations about the big city: its parks and stores and the beach.

"*¿Que onda, Dago[173]?*" I greeted my friend as he approached the lockers.

Dago was a long time friend and we played on all the school teams. We were versatile and dedicated athletes and we did well in all sports. We loved the thrill of competition.

"Are you going to San Diego on Saturday?" I asked.

"*¡Simón[174]!*" he answered excited about the trip. "*Va a estar chilo,*[175] man," Dago said. "I heard that it's the largest wrestling tournament of the state. There will be hundreds of wrestlers competing in the different weight categories.

"*Que onda[176]?*" asked John as he joined the conversation. "Did you hear the news, Lucio?" John asked laughing loudly.

"*¿Cuales nuevas, Menso?[177]*" I asked, playing along with John's teasing.

"The good news is that I'm going to San Diego," he bragged. "The bad news for you is that I will fight in the same category as you are and I'm going to kick your butt," he said threateningly.

Then he let out a loud, teasing hoot.

"I can beat you with one hand tied behind my back, stupid," I responded with a boring expression, ignoring his threat and showing my confidence.

---

[173] What's happening?

[174] Expression that means yes.

[175] It is going to be great!

[176] What is happening?

[177] What news? Stupid.

John and I had been rivals all year long. We both had the honor of wearing blue shirts, the highest award in the physical education program. We were the only two students in the whole school to perform at the highest standard in the six qualifying events: fifty yard dash, mile run, standing broad jump, pull-ups, side steps and softball throw. I was the first to get the blue shirt award but John followed within a few weeks. In wrestling, I had always defeated John but only with a very slender margin. John was always a contender and it would be unfortunate that we would have to eliminate each other in San Diego. On the other hand, we would have two opportunities to bring home a medal in a very popular weight category.

"There will be plenty of other excellent wrestlers to worry about," Mr. Belcher would tell us to cool down our argument. "Focus on the undefeated champion; he has reigned for two years.

"*Yo le voy a ganar al gringito*[178]," I would whisper to John, extending the argument.

"*No, ese guerito es mío*[179]," John replied.

"You have to go over me first," I challenged.

"I will, I will, dummy," John reassured me.

Five wrestlers and our coach, Mr. Belcher, made the journey. The coach could only take the top five wrestlers. The group was completed by Alfonso and Mike who wrestled in the lighter divisions. We all had one thing in common: sports gave us the opportunity to visit places we would never otherwise visit. Mr. Belcher said that he would take us to visit the zoo and have a picnic at Balboa Park after the tournament. He teased that he would give us a tour of San Diego whether we won or lost. He wanted our best effort while still managing to have fun. The first part of the journey to San Diego was through a thirty mile stretch of

---

[178] I am going to defeat the little Anglo.

[179] No, that white boy's mine.

barren region. This terrain was familiar to us since we were surrounded by miles of desert with lots of cactus and sand and the highway was straight as can be. Suddenly, we came to a steep mountain that rose from sea level to over four thousand feet. The climb was abrupt. The narrow highway curved sharply up the mountains and through countless sharp dips in the valleys, giving us the sensation of being on an amusement ride. A small valley at the top of the mountain was covered by white snow. Mr. Belcher said we were lucky the road was not closed at Pine Valley, a small community at the top of the mountains. I had never seen snow before, but we could not stop to touch it. We had to get to San Diego to weigh in for the tournament and we had just enough time to get there. Besides, we were not prepared for the cold and getting out of the heated car put us at risk of getting sick. It was not a day to get ill. Unfortunately, the swift change of altitude and the sudden movements caused by the dips and curves made Alfonso nauseated. Suddenly, he vomited all over Mike and Mr. Belcher who were sitting in the front. Dago, John, and I were spared. We were forced to make an unexpected stop in Pine Valley. We got off the car and rapidly cleaned it as best we could while Coach cared for Alfonso. We were lucky he had not eaten that morning because of his concern for making the weight limit of his division. The vomit was little but it stunk just the same. The rest of the trip we had to roll down our windows to disperse the strong odor. The wind was cold and by the time we reached San Diego I had fever and a strong headache. Dago complained of dizziness and also vomited before he went to weigh in. Mike and John were the healthy ones. They made fun of our frail condition. After weighing in we went to an isolated corner of the gym to lie down and try to recuperate.

The tournament was exhausting. The first elimination matches were far apart, but as the groups got smaller the matches were more frequent with short rest periods. I was lucky, since my first opponents were easy victims of my take downs and I scored a few quick matches. I had plenty of time to rest and recover from my illness. By the afternoon I was feeling better and ready to face my most difficult rivals. I reached the semifinals and waited for my next opponent. It was between John and a *gringito* from Los Angeles. Obviously, I cheered John, but I also regretted the fact that we would have to eliminate each other if he won his match. John had a very close match with his opponent, but managed to win. He jumped with joy, but he was also concerned about our match. He had just gone through a strenuous match. He knew it would be tough to eliminate me.

"*Te la rifaste, guey*[180]," I said congratulating John. "Now, I am going to have to kick your butt," I threatened.

John just smirked at me. He could not speak from exhaustion. He walked to an isolated spot to lay down and rest. *El gringito* advanced to the finals with ease. He had a chance to see John and I fight it out and wait for the victor. As expected, our match was tough. The first round, we wrestled standing, and then we flipped a coin to decide the down position on the second and third rounds. The down position meant being on your hands and knees with the other wrestler positioned behind you to try to turn you on your back to make points or win instantly with a pin; (a pin meant having both shoulders touching the ground). The wrestler in the down position would try to escape to make points and start a counter attack on the standing position. In the second round the positions would be reversed. During the first round we exchanged attacks, both neutralizing each other's offensive moves. John won the coin flip and I ended up in the down position. He tried his best to turn me on my back but was unsuccessful. Towards the end of the second round, I managed to escape from John's grasp, scoring one point. John was furious with himself. He knew that one point could mean the

---

[180] You did well, ox.

match. In the last round he tried desperately to escape, but all his efforts were in vain. I was able to hold on to the narrow margin and ended victorious, one point to zero. When I exited the wrestling mat, I turned my head towards the champion who had been witnessing the match. He seemed relaxed and confident that he would win again. I was an unknown without any previous significant tournament experience.

The finals were exciting. Every division was down to their last four wrestlers. The two winners of the semifinal would fight for first and second place. The losers would fight for a consolation prize of third and fourth place. Finally, the moment of truth for me arrived. I was unexpectedly calm when the match began. *El gringito* attacked my legs but I defended well, blocking his attack with my arms. I grabbed his arm with one hand and the back of his neck with the other, setting him up for my favorite takedown. I pushed him back. As he resisted my push, I suddenly slid my hip under his body and grabbed his neck and arm, pulling him over my back and slamming him on the mat, flat on his back. He was surprised at the swiftness of my move and the take-down gave me two points. As he struggled to get off his back, I managed to get two more points for exposing his back to the mat. In the second round he won the coin toss and I ended up in the down position. I immediately got up and escaped from his grasp and slid around his back in a well executed reversal, scoring another two points. *El campeón*[181] was furious and desperately tried to escape to no avail. I held him down until the end of the round. In the last round I was on top of the champ. In one of his attempts to escape, I exposed his back to the mat again and scored two additional points for a total of eight. When the whistle signaled the end of the round, I jumped for joy. I immediately regained composure and respectfully saluted the referee and my opponent. After I stepped

---

[181] The champion.

off the mat I ran to my coach and teammates to celebrate. It was the happiest day of my life. *Yo era el campeón*[182].

"*Ándale, ve con nosotros. No te haces nada si fallas a la escuela*[183]," my mother pleaded.

My family was going to Guadalajara for a one month vacation. It was the middle of the year and I didn't want to miss school. I had made up my mind to graduate with honors. I was doing great so far. I had made honor role in the first semester and I had brought home a gold medal from the State Junior Olympics. Going away for a month would set me back to where I would not be able to recover. I had stayed alone before and survived. I was determined to stay again. I liked the feeling of being independent. It gave me great satisfaction to be able to provide for myself and be responsible for my actions. Most of the day I was busy with my school and sport activities. On the weekends I would work harvesting asparagus to earn spending money. In the afternoons I would hang around with my friends Dago and Casey. We had many things in common. We had matured early due to our circumstances. Our parents were excessively tolerant and gave us unlimited autonomy as long as we contributed to support the family. Education was not a priority and we were not expected to become professionals. Maybe finishing high school was an adequate expectation, but it was anticipated we would end up working in the fields like everyone else in the family. Habits like

---

[182] I was the champion.

[183] Come on, go with us. Nothing will happen if you miss school.

drinking and smoking were common in our environment and we were not reprimanded when we were involved in them. Smoking was a matter of choice. Drinking was tolerated in male family members in a working environment or a celebration. I had started smoking at age eleven and had occasional drinking experiences since age twelve. It was traditional to drink a beer or two after a day of hard labor. Among field workers, it was expected of future prospects to follow the traditions. If you did not drink or smoke you were criticized and dismissed as not being a real man. *"El hombre tiene que ser cabrón*[184]," was a common phrase used by many adult males. Many young boys followed their customs in an attempt to gain acceptance *de los veteranos*[185].

Dago, Casey, and I did not hang around with our school peers. We were used to being with older people and engaged in activities many of our peers would not think of doing. We developed a bad and intriguing reputation because most students believed we lived a life of booze, parties, and girls. We were far from that, but we fed into this belief and enjoyed the status given to us. We did smoke and had occasional drinks and parties, especially when I lived by myself, but we exaggerated it to get more attention. My house was at one point known as "The Eagles' Nest" where it was alleged that we had wild parties every night. The farthest we ever went was buying a case of beer and drinking it while playing cards and telling jokes, only to wake up the next morning with a terrible hang over and making promises to God and all the saints in heaven of not ever doing it again. I have unforgettable memories of my eighth grade year. It was the best year I ever had. I graduated one of the top five students, with honors in academics and athletics. I could have been chosen the student of the year had it not been for my reputation. I wondered if it would have made a difference in the outcome of my life.

---

[184] A man is supposed to be bad.

[185] Of the veterans

I lamented myself, but I dismissed those thoughts immediately. I didn't think it would have made any difference. My destiny was manifested long before and there was nothing I could do to change it.

EL DROPOUT

A TERRIBLE HEADACHE AWOKE me early in the morning. I grabbed my head as I tried to gather my thoughts and decide what to do about my pain. I had drunk too much to ease the pain in my leg and now I had a terrible hangover. I felt like throwing up so I rushed up, limping and stumbling to the restroom. I knelt by the toilet bowl to vomit. I felt all my insides coming out. My body hurt as my muscles strained to throw out the filth from my stomach. I washed up and went to the kitchen to fix me the traditional remedy made of two tablets of Alka-Seltzer in a glass of Seven Up then I went back to my mattress to lie down. I mocked the thought of asking God and all the saints in heaven for forgiveness. I had other things to worry about. I was running out of money and Workmen's Compensation was not sending me any assistance yet. I had an appointment with my doctor soon, which could change my situation with the insurance. I was desperate. My friends had asked if I wanted to go and work. There were only two more days left in the season. The foreman had agreed to put me on the payroll and all I had to do was to be present. They all wanted to help, but I had too much pride to accept that condition. The predicament was not if I could carry on my duties but how much pain I could endure or how much damage the effort could cause my injury. The offer was appealing since the lettuce harvest was productive. The crew was cutting *carro por trio* every day. In the two days left of harvest I could earn two weeks' salary at the hourly rate.

Everyone in the crew gave me a warm greeting. We had worked together for many years and we respected each other. However, regardless of the respect they felt, I knew I would not escape their teasing. *El Poncho y el Johnny* asked me to work in their *trio* so that they could help me. They talked to me with a smirk. I was not about to let them humiliate me.

"*Ustedes no me van ayudar a mi, pendejos. Los voy a empacar en una caja*[186]," I said as we began to work.

We joked all day to forget about the hardships of the job. We knew from the start that we would work until sundown so we braced ourselves to endure the long hours. The lettuce was just the right size to cut and pack at a very fast pace but the weather was not friendly. It was wet and very cold for most of the day. The rain was slow but steady. It did not rain hard enough to stop working but it kept us damp the whole day.

"*Esta lluvia es moja pendejos*[187]," the workers would complain.

The foreman brought a bottle of liquor for each worker, to keep us warm. There were many choices to pick from. I chose a flat bottle of whiskey. It was easy to carry and one shot would warm my body and ease my pain. El Poncho, Johnny and I had worked in the same *trio* for many years in very fast crews. We always showed superiority against the other *trios*. Our harvesting skills were sharp and usually superior to most harvesters. This crew was slow, and despite my injury we did not have a problem pushing up the pace. I endured the pain under the effect of painkillers and liquor during the first day. But on the second day, the pain was so intense that I had to stop working. It was very disappointing. I lamented the outcome on the risk I had taken. I had

---

[186] You are not going to help me, stupid, I am going to pack you inside a box

[187] This rain is a stupid people dampener.

earned some money but now the pain became worse. My friends felt sorry for me but they were also concerned for themselves. They knew many of them would end up the same way. We had all experienced the wearing down of our bodies because of the harsh years as *lechugueros*. We had many battles under our belt against the weather and the bad terrain. We had all experienced the crippling pain caused by the strain of working bend over all day long.

I sat on my mattress debating my decision of returning to work. It was obvious I had worsened my injury. On the other hand, I needed the money. I questioned if I'd done right or wrong.

"What would have happened if I had money?" I asked myself. "If the insurance had sent me what I deserved, I would have stayed home and avoided the risk. *La pinchi* insurance is to blame," I reasoned angrily.

I felt that I was forced to work by the insurance company's action. Maybe I was looking for someone to blame. Perhaps I was responsible. I elected eighteen years before to become a *lechuguero*. But then again, it was a decision made due to the circumstances that surrounded my life back then.

After my successful eighth grade year, everything began to go wrong in my life. Ninth grade did not go so well. I enrolled at Calexico High school after classes had started. I was scheduled in left over classes that I did not like. I hardly knew anybody and the sensation of being the new kid in class returned. I was accepted in the school's freshman football team but because I was late I was assigned a defensive position. I argued with the coach that I had always played offense. I had been the most valuable player the previous year as a quarterback. But it was to no avail; the coach would not change his mind.

"We need a linebacker and I think you will do very well in that position. Take it or leave it," the coach said to me.

I stayed on the team, but I was not happy. To make matters worse, I was injured in the first game of the season. I sat out the rest of the season with a severely sprained ankle and a demolished ego. Later in the year, I joined the wrestling team. I had a similar outcome. The wrestling coach had several one hundred twenty pound wrestlers and decided to move me up to a higher weight category. I challenged him, but he insisted that I was the best wrestler and my sacrifice would bring essential team points throughout the season.

"This is a team and we want team effort and sacrifice to win the team championship," the coach said imposingly.

I was not happy. Again, I injured myself in the first match, abruptly ending my season. I was disappointed. I began to hate school.

At home my relationship with my father was deteriorating. The conflicts between my parents increased. My father's drinking habit was worse. I always interfered in defense of my mother. My father became more aggressive towards us and shoving matches were common. I hated these conflicts. Sometimes I got so angry that I wanted to punch my father. But I always contained myself; I did not dare do it. My mother would not allow it either. I urged my mother to separate from my father. I told her that I would drop out of school. I would work full time and support the family myself. But she could not imagine herself in a broken home and her children without a father. Divorce for women was a taboo in our culture. Many women endured domestic abuse to avoid the rejection and harassment of the people around them. These women were usually the main topic of daily gossip that included cruel stories with sexual undertones.

"*Pinchi vieja no aguanta nada. A de andar de piruja*[188]," the abnegated women would say amongst themselves to tarnish the reputation of single mothers.

---

[188] Dammed woman! She can't withstand anything. She must be a whore.

My mother had made up her mind to keep the family together regardless of the sacrifice. I was tired of it and made several threats of going away. But my mother always convinced me to stay and calm down. I did, for some time, until one day the conflict became violent. In a scuffle, my father hit me causing bruises and a bloody nose. I ran out of the house to defuse the situation. I was confused. I didn't want to hit back or injure my father. But the circumstances were forcing me to defend myself. After this incident, I did not feel safe living under the same roof with him. I moved out to live with my aunt Raquel in Mexicali. I had saved enough money to survive for a few days. Later, with my mother's support, I went to stay in Guadalajara with relatives until things calmed down. I needed time away to think of the course I needed to take in my life.

"*El prometió que va a cambiar*[189]," my mother would say to persuade me to return home.

My father always promised to change after a big conflict. He would keep his promise for a few days, giving the family peaceful times. He would not get drunk and dedicate time to the family. We would go out together to explore our surroundings. The whole family enjoyed the picnics we had in parks or camping sites. I resisted for a few days, playing the emotional blackmail game commonly used by many confused teenagers.

"*¿Qué vas a hacer? Estas muy chico, regresa a la casa*[190]," she pleaded. "*Todo va a estar bien*[191]," she promised.

I returned home within a month of my departure. I knew I was not yet ready to endure a long stay away from home. I was lacking the basics.

---

[189] He promised to change.

[190] What are you going to do? You are too young, return home.

[191] Everything is going to be alright.

I did not have a car, which was vital for work and to support myself. I still had not yet refined my abilities to harvest lettuce, a work where I could earn enough to make a decent living. I was returning home, but I had the intention to become independent soon. I made some conditions for my stay. I wanted the family to have a place to settle down and stop wandering around California after the crops. I offered to work and help raise enough money to give a down payment on our own house. I also asked to be allowed to buy my own car. My mother wanted me to return to high school, but I did not have the aspiration to go back. Having made a firm decision to work, I officially became a high school dropout at age fifteen.

Things went well at first. I worked hard to earn enough to buy my car. I worked harvesting asparagus in Imperial Valley for a couple of months. We moved to King City at the start of the lettuce harvest. We stayed at the Maggio Camp as was custom, but we were applying for a house in a new government camp just across the street that would open in a few weeks. My father soon made arrangements for me to get my first opportunity to work in his *lechuguero* crew. He was under a lot of pressure. He would have to work extra hard until I could keep up with the rest of the crew. I had some experience, but it was not enough. My father was criticized for bringing such a young lad to such a harsh job. The *veteranos* thought I would quit within a few hours.

"*Este trabajo es para hombres. Le va a tronar al morro este*[192]," the *lechugueros* would say.

It would be shameful for my father if I quit. He was risking harsh criticism for his decision of taking me to work there. I would be under the scrutinizing watch of the foreman, pressured by the rest of the crew, to make sure I was cut for the job. I was determined to prove them wrong. Initially, it was very difficult for me to keep up with my limited skills. But as the days progressed, my performance improved due to my stamina and determination to learn the trade. In a few days I gained the respect of the *veteranos*. Their criticism turned into praises. They embraced me and taught me the tricks of the trade. Soon, they accepted me as one of their own.

My father was very proud and we made a good trio for a few weeks. Our relationship began to sour after he returned to his drinking habits. He figured that since my *lechuguero* check would cover many of the expenses he could spend more of his check drinking. It was exasperating to see him drink all day at work and end up at the bar at the end of the day. He drank so much that he would just sit by a table and doze. He would gradually awake to mumble incoherent phrases. He would drink another beer and doze again. The next day he would brag about closing the bar and complain about the terrible hang over. Then he would start the cycle again by curing his illness with a beer. My father soon started to miss work something he had never done before. He had always been responsible; no matter how sick he was, he would always go to work. I tried to talk him out of drinking so much, but our conversations always

---

[192] This job is for men. (Expression that means) This boy is going to quit.

ended in heated arguments.

"*Tu no me vas a decir lo que yo haga, pendejo.   Yo soy hombre y hago lo que me da la gana, idiota*[193]," my father would snap angrily, refusing to consider anything I said.

I could not stand to see him deteriorate blinded by the denial of his alcoholism. I needed to get away from him.

---

[193] You are not going to tell me what to do, stupid. I am a man and I do what I want, you idiot.

MI CARRITO

"¿MIRA MAMÁ, TE GUSTA[194]?" I asked my mother, pointing to a nineteen-sixty-four Volkswagen, with a for sale sign, parked on the side of the road.

"*Es del campero. Dice que está muy bueno y me lo da barato*[195]," I added excitedly in an attempt to sway her to buy it for me.

My mother looked at me and smiled. She knew the car meant a lot to me, but she mildly resisted.

"*Está muy chiquito*[196]," she replied in a playful tone.

"*Está bien para mi. Yo estoy chiquito. Está echo a mi tamaño*[197]," I implored.

Si tienes razón, está de tu tamaño[198]," she agreed laughing.

At first I had problems driving *mi carrito*[199]. It had a standard transmission and I only had experience driving automatic cars. After a

---

[194] Look, mother, do you like it?

[195] It belongs to the camp caretaker. He said it is very good and he will sell it cheap.

[196] It is too small.

[197] It is OK, for me, I am small. It is made to my size.

[198] You are right, It is your size.

[199] My little car.

couple of days of cruising on Broadway, I became an expert. Most teens had cars with large motors, but *mi carrito* had a small engine. I could not compete with the other cars in fast starts when I was challenged. But, at twenty-five cents a gallon of gas, I could cruise for pennies all day long.

I did not have a driver's license, but that was a common attribute among farm workers. The only way for youngsters to get a license was through a school program. For those of us who where dropouts; it meant waiting until the age of eighteen. That did not stop me from driving all over the valley. I was not limited to the local activities anymore and I was always in search of things to do or visit. I loved to go to Pismo Beach and cruise on the sandy path along the beach. I also enjoyed picnics in Arroyo Seco or attending the dances in Watsonville. If I was surprised by nightfall far away from home, *mi carrito* became my cottage. It was small but comfortable. I always carried blankets and spare clothes, anticipating my stay.

With the means to move around, my social circle increased. It also changed. I began to distance myself from my school friends. Suddenly they appeared immature. Their conversations about parties or girls seemed childish compared to my experiences. They were constrained with their home responsibilities while I was out in the world fighting for survival. Most of my acquaintances were older people. My new peers shared similar traits: we were dropouts without a plan and trying to find an identity. We had become *lechugueros* without other aspirations. There was little attention given to other possibilities to get ahead in life. We lived day to day and did not look into the future. We were adolescents developing in an environment full of negative distractions and without proper guidance. In the intent to fit, we developed a personality that was compatible with our social circle. We were being shaped by the daily modeling of cultural myths, habits, behaviors, attitudes, feelings, and passions generated in dysfunctional families. We were fleeing from the horrors of domestic violence and abuse in our homes, only to find ourselves in a battle to subsist in the oppressive environment where farm workers lived and died.

After getting *mi carrito*, I immediately started to look for work in Salinas. Now that I had transportation, I wanted to try other lettuce companies. I wanted to test my skills against other harvesters. Initially, I had some difficulty finding a job. No one knew me and I looked very young to be a *lechuguero*. I lied about my age. I told them I was eighteen. I allowed my hair and beard to grow to give the impression that I was older. Soon, I was given the opportunity *en la Royal*, a company based in Salinas. It would be a daily, one hundred mile round trip. I would have to get up very early and get home late. I didn't mind. I avoided getting involved in home conflicts. I enjoyed driving to the fields instead of commuting. I always took my time since my car was very slow. I had to stand the shame of being passed by every car on the highway. Ironically, *mi carrito* had a limited, top speed of sixty miles an hour on flat terrain. The only time it went faster was going down hill. Unfortunately, it could slow down to twenty-five on a long, steep hill. I was fortunate that the Salinas Valley was very flat. My friends would make fun of me every chance they had.

"*Hasta los viejitos te pasan, guey*[200]," they would taunt.

Regardless of the humiliation I felt, my car had many good features. It was comfortable, efficient, hardy and economic. It consumed less than two dollars of gas on my daily journey.

"*Con cinco dólares tengo para cigarros, cerveza y gasolina, pendejos. ¿Que mas puede pedir un lechuguero*[201]?" I would reply.

My new crew was composed mainly of *Yucatecos.* They were natives of different areas of the Yucatan Peninsula. They had large heads and spoke in a strange dialect. They were distinguished for their mocking manners. *Los Yucatecos* joked all they long. They teased each other mainly about their heads and the difficulty their mothers must have had when they were born. They were usually cruel with new workers. I was not the exception. They teased me about my height, hair, beard, and *mi carrito.*

"*Se parece al dueño, chiquito y lento*[202]," They would mock me.

When I made mistakes they accused me of being lethargic. At first, I would get angry. With time, I got used to it. I learned that it was part of the *lechugero* trade, right next to booze, drugs, foul language, and

---

[200] Even the old people pass you, ox.

[201] With five dollars I have enough for cigarettes, beer and gas. What else can a lechuguero wish for?

[202] It resembles his owner, small and slow.

machismo. Novice *Lechugueros* had to deal with teasing and remain calm to gain respect in the crew.

"*Si te enojas pierdes*[203]," was the motto.

Those who were annoyed by taunting were subject to gang teasing. They became the daily prey and their day was usually miserable. Offended workers would quit and seek work somewhere else. I did not want to quit. I needed the job. I also needed to prove myself and running away like a sissy from a little teasing was not going to help.

I adapted quickly. I worked in a trio with *el Gijo*, who turned out to be an excellent teasing coach. He was a tiny man, almost a dwarf. His hands were so small he could only pack two lettuce heads at a time, instead of the normal three. He was a daily target, but he had a great repertoire with which to taunt back. In fact, as small as he was, he was the greatest teasing bully.

"*Mándalos por un tubo. Son puros mamones*[204]," he advised me when the teasing began. "Ignore them and they will leave you alone. Just smile and they will go away when they see their teasing does not bother you," he reassured me.

I followed his guidance and soon they left me alone. I even learned a few teasing phrases from *Gijo* to defend myself.

Gijo was a good worker. He knew all the tricks to be learned to be a good *lechuguero*. His size was a big handicap. His speed to work was limited. But, *Gijo* was very resourceful and was able to keep up. He was also very reliable, a trait that brought him respect. But most important of all, he was an honest person and a good friend. He took me under his wing and helped develop my *lechuguero* skills. I learned to be resourceful and use my energy wisely to improve my endurance in the harsh working environment. *Gijo* also advised me about the *lechuguero*, ambiance perils.

---

[203] If you get mad, you lose.

[204] Expression meaning: Ignore them. They are only suckers.

He told stories of good people turning bad due to their addiction to drugs, alcohol, and gambling. Many used pain, fatigue or sorrow as an excuse to experiment. In time, they became dependent and could not work without the drugs or booze.

"*Lo que se necesitan son guevos*[205]," Gijo boasted loudly, pointing at his testicles. "I don't need any chemicals in my body to be a *lechuguero*. One thing is to try it and another is to allow it to control you," he added pointing his finger at me. "*Trucha morro, póngase trucha*[206]," he insisted in soft, serious tone. "*Una cervecita, un toquecito... pssss, no hace daño una vez al año. Una no es ninguna, pero mas de dos ya son sinvergüenzadas*[207]," he chuckled.

---

[205] What is needed are balls.

[206] Expression meaning, careful, boy, be careful.

[207] One beer, a joint, psss is not bad for you once a year. One is nothing, more than two is being irresponsible.

MARÍA ELENA

"*Levántate hijo, se té hace tarde*[208]," my mother called me early one morning to go to work.

As I was getting ready, I was startled by a loud door slam coming from the neighboring house. It was María Elena's house. I went to a window facing her house and listened on a loud argument. Through the window, I had a fuzzy view of the living room, but the argument was taking place to one side and I could not see the perpetrators. The voices were familiar: it was María Elena and her brother Roberto.

"*Habré la puerta Elena. Sal de inmediato. Hazle caso a mi padre*[209]," Roberto demanded.

"*Ya té dije que no*[210]," María Elena shouted back.

"*Se nos hace tarde para el trabajo. Mi padre esta furioso, te va a ir peor si no sales*[211]," Roberto insisted in a threatening voice.

"*Ya lárgate y déjame en paz. A mí no me importa nada*[212]," she

---

[208] Get up, son; you're going to be late.

[209] Open the door, Elena. Come out immediately. Listen to my father.

[210] I said no.

[211] It is getting late for work. My father is furious; you will get it worse if you don't come out.

[212] Leave now and leave me alone. I do not care about anything.

131

retaliated aggressively. *"No voy a trabajar y me vale madre*[213]," María Elena shouted.

"Ya vámonos, hay que se quede," angrily shouted their father, *Don Polo.*

I heard two loud, car door slams, screeching of tires as they sped off and then silence.

I was impressed. María Elena had stood up to male authority in her home. She had refused to be the subject of disregard and abuse embedded in many family traditions towards their female members. The father was a tyrant who forced his children to miss school to work, taking one-week turns and repeating the cycle throughout the year. I had heard some of my sister's conversations and learned of María Elena's discontent. To actually confront her father, it was truly impressive.

"Parece una potranquita[214]," I thought to myself, with a grin. *"Así como a mi me gustan, chiquitas pero picosas*[215]," I murmured with an unexpected sensation.

I reflected on the incident all day long. I felt proud of María Elena for her courage, but I was concerned about the outcome of her defiance. "She will surely be punished," I thought, alarmed by the possible consequences. Defiance was dealt with corporal punishment in many families. It was the means to intimidate and control insubordination among members of the family, especially women. I got off work early that day, and unlike others, I hurried home. A new instinct urged me to avoid delays and get back promptly. I made some excuses to my friends to get away without creating suspicion. When I got there, I was pleased to see Silvia and María Elena chatting in the living room. They had just

---

[213] I am not working and I don't give a damn.

[214] She looks like a young wild mare.

[215] Just the way I like them, small but spicy.

arrived from school and were having a snack.

"*Hola, que onda*[216]?" I meekly greeted.

My sister looked at me astonished.

"*¿Qué milagro que nos saludas*[217]? She asked sarcastically, emphasizing the word "*nos*".

María Elena returned my greeting with a smile.

"*¿Como estas Lucio*[218]?" she said amicably.

I felt guilt. I did not know what to say and unexpectedly began to stutter an explanation about my changed attitude towards her. María Elena's proximity made me nervous. She was enchanting and I felt so grimy and undeserving. I opted for excusing myself to shower and change clothes. My sister looked at me with a sinister grin. María Elena's look was gentle, accepting my pretext as I left the room. I took a quick shower and changed clothes. I retired to my room and laid down to rest. I purposely left the door partially open and positioned myself to admire María Elena. I pretended to be reading and occasionally looked over the book trying to attract her attention. She must have felt my stare since she looked my way, her eyes meeting mine. Filled with emotion, I cupped my lips and blew her a kiss. Her smile broadened as she looked away.

I was the happiest *lechuguero* the next day. With a smiling expression, I sang love songs all day. I ignored my friends' teasing games and or conversations, focusing on my thoughts. I could not understand what have gotten into me. One day I hated her guts and now I could not get her out of my mind. I was confused about her reaction towards my approach. I felt she was attracted to me, but what if she was being

---

[216] Hi, what is happening?

[217] What a miracle that you greet us.

[218] How are you, Lucio?

deceitful? At times I was concerned; she could be conspiring with my sister to avenge my arrogance. I had snubbed María Elena for so many years. What made me think she would want to be around me? I was hesitant to ask her out.

"What if she rejects me? I would be miserable," I mumbled to myself.

I would pick any flower on my path to pull its petals to see if she loved me or not. Usually the petal pulling ended in "she loves me" and I rejoiced over the outcome with a love song.

"*Mari es mi amor. Solo con ella vivo la felicidad*[219]," I chanted loudly.

"*Este guey está enamorado. De cincho anda con una jaina*[220]," Gijo said with disdain.

"*¿Nos estas mandando por un tubo por una vieja, péndejo*[221]?" my friends would blast when I excused myself to go home early.

María Elena's unexpected reaction caused an impression in her family also. Her father had grounded her, but refrained from beating her. She was allowed to finish her eighth grade year and attend the graduation. But she was always under heavy surveillance. The only way to speak to her now was when the parents were at work or when she was coming from school. I committed to arrive early from work to stand vigil for an opportunity to speak to her. I kept a watchful eye for her. On occasions, I would see her silhouette through the window as I spied quietly, trying to figure out what she was doing. My heart pounded with excitement when I saw her walk out of her house. She went to their station wagon to get some bags and quickly returned inside. I lost sight of her. I waited to see if I saw her again but it was in vain. I went to my room and rested

---

[219] Mari is my love. I live happiness only with her.

[220] This ox is in love. He is probably going around with a chick.

[221] Expression meaning: Are you ignoring us for a woman, stupid?

on my bed. I was thinking of what to say to her. I was determined to ask her out, but I did not want to expose my true feelings. I did not want to be heart broken. I had the reputation of being flirtatious and was elected the biggest flirt in school. I did not want to have a long-term relationship with any girl. María Elena was aware and it concerned me. I would cautiously take the risk. Suddenly, I heard a noise coming from the living room. It was my sister and María Elena talking. I could not believe she was in my house. I spied through the partially opened door and listened in on their conversation. Her father had gone on an errand and she snuck out for a few minutes. This gave me an opportunity to speak with her and once and for all, extinguishing my doubts. I saw my sister walk to the kitchen and I came out of hiding, trying to make myself visible. I tried to make it look unintentional but María Elena's immediate attention made me feel like I was the one under surveillance.

"*¿Hola, como estas?*" I greeted.

After a few preliminary exchanges about school and work, I impulsively asked her to go out with me.

"We can have some fun together," I said, trying to hide my real feelings.

I wanted to make it seem liked it was a casual request and not a torrential manifestation of love.

"I am grounded. My father will not let me go anywhere," she responded.

"Well, what about later, when you are allowed to go out?" I insisted.

"¡Uuuuu!" she said melodiously. "That is not going to happen in a long time," she said.

"Well, can we at least talk?" I asked.

María Elena smiled and agreed. She excused herself as she hurried out the door towards her house. She went in just as her father parked on the curve. I went to my room still puzzled about the exchange. The outcome was not clear. She agreed to speak to me but she had not committed to have a relationship.

"How stupid of me, I didn't really ask her!" I reproached myself. I didn't say, "María Elena, will you be my girlfriend?"

I whispered it softly pretending she was in front of me.

She sat on the low, wooden fence that outlined the front yard of the cabins, pretending to look down the street. María Elena knew I was spying behind the curtains. As soon as I saw her, I came out and walked towards her. She smiled and turned her attention towards me. We exchanged greetings and spoke casually for a few minutes. As I became confident, the conversation became more intimate. I gathered courage and finally asked the question.

"*¿Quieres ser mi novia*, María Elena[222]?" I asked romantically.

She hesitated, taking my proposition into consideration.

"*¿Qué no tienes novia*[223]?" she asked.

"No," I responded.

"Maybe you just want to play with me," she debated.

She looked at me with a smile as I pleaded my case. We looked into each other eyes and stood silently for a long time. There was no need for words. The attraction was mutual, the feelings obvious by our demeanor, it was love. We held hands and walked a few feet to the laundry building in search of privacy. Inside the empty building we embraced and put our lips together in a passionate kiss.

"Is this a yes?" I asked as I caressed her hair.

She smiled and kissed me with tenderness.

"*Si, Lucio, quiero ser tu novia*[224]," she said with a soothing smile.

Suddenly, the magic moment was broken by the sudden slam of a

---

[222] Do you want to be my girlfriend, María Elena?

[223] Don't you have a girlfriend?

[224] Yes Lucio, I want to be your girlfriend.

door. María Elena's mother came through the laundry door steaming, shouting threats and insults at her. The mother tried to slap María Elena, but she evaded her and left in haste, more embarrassed than afraid of the consequences. The mother turned at me and told me to stay away and threatened to tell *Don Polo*. I stood silent for a few minutes not knowing what to do, and then I walked out and went home confused at the hastiness of the events. One moment I was in heaven tasting the warmth of her lips and another, I was alone and worried for the well-being of my dear María Elena.

Our relationship did not go well initially. Her curfew was strict. Her father's restrictions severely limited our opportunities to be together. She was not allowed to go anywhere by herself. Her brothers would pick her up at school, chaperone her to the theater and keep watch when she went outside. It infuriated me to see other boys courting her. One of her brothers tried to impose his friend on María Elena to distract her from me. Annoyed, I confronted her brother Roberto for his pestering. I threatened to kick his butt. It was exasperating, living next door and not being able to speak to her. I began to distance my self from María Elena and frequent other acquaintances.

I opened the door to answer a soft knock. It was María Elena inquiring for Silvia. I greeted her and asked her to come in. We spoke for a few minutes and went to sit outside on the fence. She was concerned that her father or brothers would see her at my house.

"You have not looked for me lately," she said bitterly. "I see you are very busy riding with those *gordas*[225]. Aren't you afraid they will break your little car?" she taunted.

"They are just friends," I protested.

"Would you like it if I went out with friends?" she questioned.

María Elena was rightfully upset and wanted to break up. I sadly

[225] Fat girls.

realized, I was about to lose her because of my selfish behavior. I wanted María Elena to sacrifice for our relationship while I continued a life of pleasure and unfaithfulness. I pleaded for a new opportunity. I asked to formalize our relationship with her parents. I offered to speak to her father for permission to court her. But she was concerned about asking her father. He would use it as an excuse to reproach her abnegated mother. Despite María Elena's objections, I went to her house and spoke with *Don Polo*. After a wave of insults towards María Elena and a severe criticism about me, he reluctantly agreed. *Don Polo* questioned why her daughter had eyes for a Mexican hippy that acted like a *pachuco*[226]. He accused me of being filthy because of my excessive facial hair. I knew the insults and criticism were coming, but I remained calm to avoid a confrontation. Reluctantly, *Don Polo* gave his permission for my visits; he agreed for me to speak with María Elena in front of the house. But he prohibited us to meet anywhere else. His conditions were unreasonable, but we accepted. We did not have another choice; it was better than nothing. At least now we could spend our afternoons together hoping for more leniencies in the future. Despite the limitations we enjoyed ourselves. We spent many beautiful moments holding hands under the moon and stars; sharing love phrases amongst countless suspires. The hours would fly when we were together.

I began to get impatient about my relationship with María Elena. I was longing to have her with me at all times, to kiss her and hold her in my arms. I wanted to go out, dance, go to the theater or walk on the beach like a normal couple. I hated the way she was treated at home. We were not completely happy. As our situation became desperate, I urged María Elena to elope with me. She refused.

"My mother would be persecuted by my father for the rest of her

---

[226] Gang member.

life," she said frantically. "I don't want to see her suffer the hell my father will put her through because of my actions," she added seeking my understanding.

I agreed, but we needed to find a solution to the unbearable experience we were going through. The severe limitations to our relationship were unfair. I was resourceful enough to sustain a home by myself and I was willing to commit to a long term relationship and start our own family.

"Would you marry me?" I proposed passionately. "I will love you and care for you for the rest of my life," I promised.

"*Sí*," she said, holding my hand.

She embraced me, seeking refuge in my arms. I kissed her lips with tenderness and devotion, sealing our commitment. We agreed that I

would speak to her father as soon as possible.

Don Polo was walking across the street alone smoking a cigarette when I approached him; his demeanor did not intimidate me. I was prepared for his arrogance and fury. I knew I was the last man he wanted his younger daughter to marry, but María Elena and I had resolved to take this issue to the extremes. I respectfully asked him for her hand in marriage. He rudely dismissed my proposal. He snapped at me with a flurry of insults.

"*Tu eres un pendejo. Tu palabra no vale. Eres un mocoso inútil que no gana ni para rasurarse*[227]," he ranted. "*Que venga tu padre a responder por ti. Esa es la tradición*[228]," he said offended by my request

He walked away livid, mumbling insults and threats. I walked home disappointed at the outcome of our short and nasty conversation. I had contained myself and respected *Don Polo's* reaction, but he was wrong considering me unworthy of his daughter. I was offended by his rejection and lack of acknowledgement of my ability to support María Elena.

"¡*Yo tengo huevos*[229]!" I mumbled to myself.

I was a *lechuguero* and no matter what he thought, I earned more than him, enough to support a family. Disenchanted I went home in search of my mother's support. I knew that my father would refuse to ask for my girl's hand. To my surprise, my mother initially denied me her support.

"*Estas muy chico*[230]," she said.

I explained don Polo's attitude and begged her to speak to my father. She refused saying that I was a going through a temporary phase, that I was confused about my feelings and that in a few days it would all go away. Her rejection only increased my determination and I proceeded to confront my father.

"*Estas pendejo*[231]! My father snapped at me. "*Son unos escuincles que no saben limpiarse el rabo y se quieren casar*[232]," he argued.

I became irate and started arguing with both my mother and father.

---

[227] You are stupid. Your word is worthless. You are just a brat that cannot earn enough money to shave.

[228] Let your father come and respond for you. That is the tradition.

[229] I have balls!

[230] You are too small.

[231] You are stupid!

[232] You are brats that don't know how to clean your butt and you want to marry.

I used emotional blackmail by threatening to elope to a place where they would never see me again. I went out slamming the door and driving away *en mi carrito*.

The next day, my father crossed the street with a six-pack under his arm towards *Don Polo's* house. My blackmail had persuaded my mother to back me up. She must have somehow convinced my father to speak to *Don Polo*. I did not accompany my father; I did not want to hear what they had to say. Rumors had already spread in the camp about the possible causes of our hasty marriage. The gossip was cruel. The residents rumored that I was a pedophile, since María Elena's appearance was that of a very young girl. They were certain she was pregnant and our parents were trying to amend it with a marriage. No one believed we could support ourselves and many jokes were told about our parents having to support us. There was one thing they were all sure of, that our marriage would not last more than two months. No one entertained the possibility that we were in love, that we wanted to be independent and form our own family. Now more than ever, we wanted to get married and show everyone that we were serious and responsible enough to care for ourselves. I would work diligently to cover the wedding expenses and our honeymoon. My pride would not allow me to receive assistance from anyone. I pledged to be the sole supporter for my family without expecting assistance from my wife or children. María Elena would care for our home and children. We were committed to giving our children a better environment than the ones María Elena and I had experienced.

THE WEDDING

THE TAXI DRIVER NERVOUSLY mumbled a series of obscenities as he was pulled over by the police. He had driven into a one way street in front of a cop.

"*¡Qué pendejo! No vi al pinchi chota*[233]," the driver snapped, banging the steering wheel of the taxi with his fists. "*Me va a chingar este guey*[234]," he added in concern.

I sat in the back seat sweating profusely, looking at my watch nervously. I was already delayed by the unexpected mechanical failure of Fidencio's car. The transmission failed precisely when we were heading to church. And now, with this holdup, I was not going to make it on time for my long-awaited wedding ceremony.

"María Elena must be very concerned," I thought anxiously. "Everything had gone so well, up to now. Why is this happening?" I asked myself confused at my misfortune.

The four months leading to the wedding had gone smoothly. At first, I had to separate myself from María Elena to follow the lettuce harvest to Bakersfield. But soon, we were together again in Calexico

---

[233] How Stupid! I did not see the dam cop.

[234] This ox is going to screw me.

where we began the wedding preparations. We were forced to marry in Mexicali. We were only sixteen and in California the legal age was eighteen. In Mexicali, the presence of our parents was enough. We made all the arrangements for the wedding there. Maria Elena searched for her wedding dress and all the complements, while I arranged the essentials for the celebration. We planned a small celebration and saved our money to spend on our honeymoon.

The civil ceremony had turned out to be a humorous event. As we inquired for information, a door opened suddenly, and the judge stormed in the office.

"¿Donde esta la pareja[235]?" he anxiously asked the secretary.

The secretary shrugged her shoulders.

"Se ha de haber rajado este pinchi morro[236]," nagged the annoyed judge.

The judge's chamber was full of elementary students. They had come to witness a marriage between minors which had been arranged by the judge. The judge paced up and down the hall thinking of a solution. Then, he noticed us. He asked the secretary about our inquiry. When he found out we were a couple of minors who wanted to tie the knot, he proposed to marry us immediately. We were the solution to his problem. It didn't matter who he married as long as it was a couple of minors. We were not expecting anything like this. We were not dressed appropriately and we had not brought witnesses. The judge didn't care. He advised my father to get someone from a nearby bar.

"Just offer them a couple of beers," said the judge humorously.

He had found the solution for his problem and such small details were not going to ruin it for him. We entered the chamber under the curious look of the students and teachers who were waiting for the

---

[235] Where is the couple?

[236] This damn kid must have back down.

ceremony to begin. The judge modified the ceremony to explain to the students the implications of matrimony. The ceremony was a memorable event. Looking back at my pictures, it was funny how we blended in the multitude of students standing in the background to see. We were not much older than they were and it was difficult to identify us as the newlyweds. María Elena and I were very happy to have overcome the first requirement in such a unique way. But now, I was in danger of missing the religious ceremony.

I began to panic about the delay. I saw the officers and the driver argue endlessly as the minutes inevitably vanished away. I became restless. I got off the taxi and approached one of the officers.

"*Pásanos quebrada*[237]," I pleaded.

I explained how desperate I was to get to the church and how the driver was only trying to help me. The officer listened with amazement as I told how Fidencio, my best man, was driving me to church when his car had malfunctioned. I had become stranded and in desperation, I flagged down the taxi. The driver had one passenger to deliver and then he would become free to take me. The officer was sympathetic with my situation and offered to help. Laughing, he ordered the taxi driver to follow the patrol car to the church. They would deal with the driving infraction there. The officers joked about doing their good deed of the day by helping me get to church, as soon as possible, so I would "hang myself". The officer turned the siren on and dashed through down town running through all the red lights. The driver followed closely; I was twenty minutes late when I arrived.

"*¿Donde estabas pendejo*[238]?" asked my father frantically.

I ignored his insults, rushed out the taxi, and ran to María Elena's car. She was seated in the back crying. Her distress was compounded by

---

[237] Give us a break.

[238] Where were you stupid?

the insistence of the priest that I had stood her up.

"*No, ése jovencito ya se dio a la fuga*[239]," the priest constantly repeated.

María Elena had endured nerve-racking minutes; tormented by her father's nagging about the embarrassment my actions were causing the family. *Don Polo* assured I had backed down and insisted that they leave immediately. María Elena resisted her father's demands, believing I would not stand her up. Her persistence paid off. It gave me time to arrive and continue with our commitment. We embraced as I explained what had happened. I pleaded with the priest to reconsider the situation and despite my delay, to go through with the ceremony. The priest agreed to perform a short ceremony since he had another couple waiting after us. Among harsh speculation and criticism, we carried on with the wedding. It was short but sweet. María Elena looked lovely in her wedding gown. Wiping off her tears, she walked down the isle as I waited at the altar. Her mixed emotions were cleared as we exchanged bows. Her smile was visible behind her veil when we exchanged rings. She trembled with emotion when I uncovered her face and tenderly kissed her forehead. Finally, after a frantic episode and against all **odds, we had gained the freedom to be together.**

---

[239] No, that young man escaped.

The caravan of honking cars left the church to the residence where the celebration took place. The celebration was simple but cozy. Only a few friends and family members gathered at a large home volunteered by a friend for the after party. Putting aside the blasphemies about the incident, we ate, drank, and danced for a few hours. We tried to forget all the conflicts we had gone though in the last months. Everyone opposed our marriage for different reasons. Some were sympathetic but foresaw conflict and advised us to wait.

"If you truly love each other you will have the resolve to wait," Mr. Belcher would tell me. "Enjoy life, finish school, don't rush your decision," he advised.

Our parents tried to convince us to change our minds, one day with promises of long vacations or a new car, another, with threats of denying us their help if we failed. But we were committed. We tried to enjoy ourselves by following some of the wedding traditions, but in reality, María Elena and I wanted to leave and enjoy our solitude.

Finally it was time. Turning the car ignition it made a clicking sound. With a frown, I tried again with the same results. I looked out the window startled, I saw my friends mocking me.

"*Este guey esta embrujado. Carro que tienta carro que chinga*[240]," they taunted.

I could not believe my misfortune; even *mi carrito* was conspiring against me. It had always been reliable, and now as María Elena and I were getting ready to leave the celebration, *mi carrito* would not start! Everyone stopped waving good-bye and started laughing. I looked at María Elena with a cunning smile. With determination, I put the transmission in neutral, got off the car and started pushing. I wanted to get the car moving, jump inside, and then shift the transmission into first gear to force the motor to start. I could not get enough speed on my first attempt and the car stalled. My friends were amused and made all kinds of sly remarks. They teased about all the cars conspiring against my urgency to leave.

"¡*Subete guey*[241]!" they shouted. Three of my friends pushed the car until it had enough speed for the motor to start. As the car started, I pressed hard on the accelerator, making the tires of *mi carrito* skid. I made a u-turn and made a victory lap around the street honking the claxon among the cheers of my family and friends.

"*Dale guey, dale, no se té vaya a parar*[242]," they shouted with burlesque remarks.

I sped off through the dark and dusty streets of the neighborhood and headed for our love nest. Finally, after a prolonged agony came the ecstasy of having my beloved María Elena by my side.

---

[240] This ox is bewitched; car that he touches, car that he breaks.

[241] Get on ox.

[242] Go, ox, don't let it stop.

THE MARRIAGE

"It must be her," I thought as I rushed to answer the phone.

It was a collect call from María Elena, which I declined. It was a strategy we used to communicate. María Elena would make a collect call, as a signal for me to call back to speak with her. She had limited access to a phone and a call from California to Mexico was less expensive. I was so happy to hear from her and the kids. I had encouraging news about my injury. I had gone to a doctor of my choice, not related to the insurance. His diagnostic favored my request for worker's compensation benefits. He was treating my injury and alleviating my pain. The doctor also advised me of other economic assistance I could apply for when María Elena returned. She questioned with concern about my pain and the difficulty I must be having all alone. I tried to sound cheerful to avoid worrying her. But in reality, I wish she was back. I needed her caresses. I was dependent on her for my needs and my healing. She had always been my support in good and bad times. From the very first day of marriage our life had been full of challenges. The honeymoon ended and real life began. It was a hard awakening, returning from the delights of paradise to the hardships of the *lechuguero* life.

Our ignorance of the responsibilities as a couple was obvious. We had to learn together the hard way. Our first lessons were about learning to live independently. We did not even have an idea where to start. Our first blunder was not securing housing for our return. The consequence was to live with my in-laws until we found our own apartment. We were back to the restrictive environment we were fighting to get rid of and we had to prolong independence for a few more weeks. We accepted the offer reluctantly only to find it rather convenient since María Elena did not know how to cook. At first we did not see any inconvenience when we talked about it.

"I will survive only off love and a bologna sandwich." I teased her.

Soon we found out that cooking is an important trait a *lechuguero's* wife must have. It was part of the traditional responsibilities of the farm-working women. Among these families, it was a dishonor not to cook.

"*Pa'que sirve una pinchi vieja que no sabe cocinar*[243]?" the abnegated women would gossip at the laundry and in the fields.

María Elena had not learned the skills of a housewife. She rebelled against her mother when given house tasks. Now that she was facing a new responsibility, she had to start from scratch.

When I returned to work, I needed my daily *lonche*[244] and Maria Elena did not have a clue how to make it.

"*Yo te enseño a hacerle lonche a Lucio*[245]," *Doña* Bernardina offered my wife.

The women would get up earlier to prepare the day's meals. At two in the morning, María Elena, her sister, and their mother were engulfed making food and tortillas. Later they would wrap a generous amount of tacos for breakfast and fill thermos with hot food for lunch. *Doña* Bernardina was an excellent cook; I was fortunate she was teaching Maria Elena.

---

[243] What good is dam broad that does not cook?

[244] Lunch

[245] I will teach you how to make lunch for Lucio.

My friends envied me and constantly pointed out my good fortune. When they came to pick me up for work, María Elena would walk me to the door and kiss me good-bye as she handed me *mi lonche*. When I returned, she would meet me at the door with a passionate kiss.

"*¡Que suerte la de éste guey[246]!*" they would say enviously.

"*Se rallo, se encontró una jaina bien chula y buena para hacer refín[247],*" said one friend, assuming my wife cooked the food.

"*Y lo despiden con un beso. ¿Qué mas puede pedir un lechuguero[248]?*" said another.

They ended teasing each other about being sent to work with a frown and a cold *lonche* or a sandwich.

"*¿A ti que te echó la fiera[249]?*" they would ask each other mockingly.

Many peers praised my lonche. Some always sat to eat with me knowing I had plenty of soft, flour tortillas and delicious *tacos* to share. They complimented *mi salsa picante* [250] and the variety of desserts I always found neatly wrapped in aluminum foil.

"*A éste si lo quieren y le hacen lonche con cariño[251],*" my friends would compliment as they shared my food. They said my wife made the best tortillas in the world. The attention I received because of my *lonche* was good. I enjoyed it. A lechuguero with a good *lonche* is always welcomed.

"*Siéntate con nosotros[252],*" said Jose, a member of my *trio*.

I meekly declined his offer. I had been avoiding my friends all day

---

[246] What luck this ox has!

[247] He lucked out; he married a pretty gal and great at making food.

[248] And they send him off with a kiss. What else can a lettuce harvester ask for?

[249] What did your fiend gave you?

[250] My hot sauce.

[251] They do love him and make his lunch with love.

[252] Sit with us.

long. It was the first time my wife made my lunch by herself and I sadly discovered that it was far from being like the *lonches* of the last few weeks. The tortillas were hard and crumbled when rolled into a taco. The first bite of my tacos was like biting a rock. The food was salty and hardly edible. I was afraid to be ridiculed by my friends when they found out the reality of my *lonches*. It was inevitable; I could not hide it forever. Jose walked to me and asked for a tortilla. He grabbed it and immediately noticed they were not the same. The tortilla was shaped like a baby's bib. Jose put the tortilla on his chest and modeled it to the rest of the crew to amuse them.

"*Ya se me hacia mucha suerte la de este guey*[253]," José said making fun of me.

Everyone around me started to laugh and make jokes. I was the laughing stock of the crew for the next days to come. I was upset about the whole deal. I felt betrayed by María Elena. I felt she was slacking off in her responsibilities. Her carelessness had brought shame to my name. I became angry and wanted to get home to protest.

"*¿Qué chingados paso con mi pinchi lonche*[254]?" I complained angrily about all the shame the lunch had brought me.

I did not accept María Elena's excuses and verbally harassed her. At first she apologized, but soon she got tired of my whining and retaliated.

"*A mi no me vas a gritar*[255]," she said offended. "*Yo no soy tu criada y si no te gusta busca otra*[256]," she said sobbing.

She went into the bedroom crying and left me standing talking to myself. When she disappeared slamming the door, I realized I had

---

[253] I always felt it was too much luck for this ox.

[254] What the hell happened with my dam lunch?

[255] You are not going to shout at me.

[256] I am not your maid and if you don't like it go find another.

just created our first serious argument. I began to feel guilty and tried to console her. But María Elena would not listen to my pleading and I ended up spending my first night sleeping on the couch. The next day was miserable. I had to make my own bologna sandwiches and my sadness was apparent, giving the *lechugueros* a reason to tease me.

"*Me van a dar carrilla todo el día*[257]," I lamented.

La carrilla [258]from my peers was cruel. They mimicked my wife throwing a bag of bread and a pack of bologna and telling me, "Make your own lunch."

"*¿Dormiste con el perro, guey*[259]?" they asked.

I took all the *carrilla* quietly. I returned home sadly and repented. María Elena was not speaking to me despite my apologies and promises of never doing it again. I insisted throughout the afternoon and finally gained forgiveness later that night. We went out to eat and returned holding hands and smiling. The reconciliation temporarily eased the tension in our relationship. It was one of many more to come.

Through the years, our relationship was put through difficult trials. My immaturity and lack of good judgment created many problems. Our relationship shifted abruptly from pleasant to turbulent. Elena's tolerance made our reconciliations possible, but I always found reasons to raise her stress. I began to develop the same behaviors I was running from. I became controlling, manipulative, and abusive like my father and *Don Polo*. I neglected my family to portray the image of *muy macho*[260] with the other *lechugueros*. Older couples said that all couples had problems and that conflicts were part of marriage. María Elena and I had our good share of a conflictive life.

---

[257] They are going to tease all day long.

[258] The teasing.

[259] Did you sleep with the dog, ox?

[260] Tough man.

MAMACITA

"I AM SORRY DARLING, but your mother has to come with your little brother," said the elderly nurse to María Elena, advising her of the doctor's office rules.

"But I am the mother," replied María Elena.

"How can it be? You don't look older than twelve," said the nurse, amazed at María Elena's claim.

"Actually, I am sixteen and my baby was born two weeks ago in this hospital. I have an appointment for his check-up," explained María Elena.

"You are such a tiny thing," said the nurse in a sweet tone as she peeked under the blanket to see the baby.

Suddenly, she looked up at me standing behind María Elena.

"Are you the father?" she asked, disgusted.

My appearance made me look older and gave the impression that I had taken advantage of María Elena. With long hair and untrimmed beard I looked like a beast; she was petite and looked so innocent.

"Yes," I said proudly. "He looks just like me," I added sarcastically.

The elderly nurse ignored my comments and continued to compliment María Elena for her baby.

"You did a great job, honey," she said as she added our son's name to the waiting list.

"María Elena and I sat in a small waiting room. She was still weak from the birth. The baby was born with some complications. He was born prematurely and weighed only five pounds and six ounces, but after a few days in the incubator and the doctor's intensive care, Lucito was healthy. We enjoyed showing our baby around. We would take him with us everywhere we went. It caught the attention of people who were always curious about María Elena's age. We liked the compliments. We were both very happy that our dream of becoming parents had come true. But soon we found out that having a baby was not a dream but a real task.

The first night we brought him home, the loud cries of the baby woke me up. I raised my head from the pillow and saw María Elena in the kitchen. I stumbled out of bed and went to her side. She was preparing a bottle of formula.

"Let me help you. You shouldn't get up. When you need something, wake me up," I said.

"I didn't want to wake you up yet. It is only two in the morning and you can still rest another two hours before you go to work," María Elena replied.

"No, I want you to rest," I insisted.

The baby continued to cry until María Elena gave him his bottle. Half asleep, I held the baby in my arms and paced up and down the room until he went to sleep. It was a routine that was repeated every day for months. That beautiful and peaceful baby had turned into a nightmare. He would sleep during the day and wake up at two in the morning crying desperately. There were times when we were very worried about the baby's health and María Elena asked our mothers for advice. They both said that the baby's behavior was normal.

"*¿Querían tener hijo? Pues ahora se aguantan*[261]," was the most common answer from our mothers.

We did not know what to expect, and every time Lucito cried we worried. On several occasions we took him to the hospital late at night. The diagnostics were constipation or stomachache. Most of the time, the baby was just hungry or wanted to be held in our arms. We learned the hard way that babies required more than just showing them around.

María Elena and I had agreed to share the responsibilities of our marriage in order to avoid some of the unfair conditions our mothers had endured. We agreed that she would take care of our children and the house chores while I worked to provide for the expenses of our home. I could never conceive her working in the fields. Taking care of the children would be a difficult task in itself. It required more skills then we had anticipated. Lucito's birth was a rude awakening.

I became a good provider. I took care of all my family's needs. But I was selfish and rejected any opinions or ideas that differed from my own. Contradictions were confronted with intimidating tactics. María Elena's protests were met with tantrums. She became insecure and abnegated and tolerated my temper. But when I exceeded her tolerance level,

---

[261] You wanted to have a son? Well now don't complain.

she defended herself. She responded aggressively and used emotional blackmail by threatening to leave with our child to where I would never see them again. She knew my vulnerable spot and I always ended up seeking reconciliation. Despite many years of turmoil we salvaged our marriage. But unconsciously, our continuous confrontations depleted our children's already underprivileged environment.

LOS SAIKONEROS

My Lechuguero friends came to pay their regard when they heard I had been injured. They came in the afternoons, after work. They would bring beer and we would spend hours chatting in the backyard. We had formed a tight social group while working in a well-known lettuce company. They had earned the nickname *Saikoneros*[262] because of their endurance working in one of the toughest companies in Imperial Valley. We had many years of loyal service, in severe conditions under this company, only to lose our jobs after a long and violent labor struggle. I was one of the youngest workers and worked for eleven years with *los Saikoneros*. Many of the Saikoneros had spent most of their lives working for this company. The experiences we shared during that time maintained our ties for many years to come.

I initially applied for work with this company in search of a stable source of employment in order to save enough for the summer. The company had a reputation of working its people hard throughout the season. It was hard to undergo, but the paychecks were good. We also made enough credit to qualify for the highest unemployment benefits for the long summer. The Saikoneros had a reputation for having

---

[262] Workers of a company named Saikon.

159

strong endurance and determination to work under extreme weather conditions. Many people who were not used to extreme conditions would quit within a few days and never return.

"*Están locos esos gueyes, trabajan hasta lloviendo*[263]," said the critics of the working habits of the company. I also wanted to work with *los Saikoneros* because I wanted to fulfill my goal of becoming a respected *lechuguero*. Keeping up with the best *lechugueros* in the valley would bring me the recognition I was looking for.

Initially it was difficult to adapt to the *Saikonero* routine. But a friend of mine, Jose, helped me make a smooth transition. Jose was a notorious *lechuguero* and had influence in the crew. He invited me and showed me how to evade intimidation from *Los Saikoneros*.

"*Te van a querer tronar*[264]," he teased. "*No te agüites. Yo te hago un paro*[265]," he said.

It was nice to have someone to advocate for you in such a hostile environment.

On my first day, I sat quietly on the bus waiting for the departure to the lettuce field. It was two in the morning, yet the streets were full of people rushing to work. The commute to the work site was very long at the start of the season. In the bus, workers would chat softly while others curled up in their seat trying to sleep. Jose did not ride the bus to work so I sat by myself under the curious eyes of *los veteranos*. Suddenly, a large man called "*La Leona*[266]" entered the bus insulting everyone. His greetings were reminders of their mother's defects. His swearing was answered with insults followed by booing.

---

[263] These ox are crazy, they work even in the rain.

[264] They will try to make you blow.

[265] A phrase meaning: Don't worry I will help you.

[266] The Lioness.

"*Cállate el hocico pinchi Leona*[267]," said some angry workers.

La Leona threatened everyone as he walked the aisle, cussing at curled up workers pretending to sleep.

"*Ya están viejos*[268]," he shouted. "*Ya se habían de pensionar*[269]," he sneered.

La Leona stopped by my seat and looked at me in dismay.

"*¿Y este guey quien es*[270]?" he asked, pointing at me.

I stared in silence. He towered over me as I remained seated. He snapped a box of cigarettes from my shirt pocket and took one. He lighted the cigarette, took one puff and threw the box back at me.

"*Vale mas que te la rifes guey, porque sino aquí vas a tronar*[271]," he threatened me. *¿Quién trajo este guey*[272]? He asked.

"*Ya cállate el hocico pinchi Leona. Deja ese morro en paz*[273]," said an angry man sitting behind me.

"*Tu no te metas pinchi Yuca*[274]," said *La Leona*.

La Yuca was a small *veterano* well respected by everyone. He had been a boxer, held a black belt in Judo, and had been a *Saikonero* for many years.

"*Si sigues chingando te voy partir la madre pinchi mariguano*[275]," said *La Yuca* as he stood up and threw a sharp kick, brushing *Leona's* butt.

"*Pinchi cuerpo de oquis*[276]," *La Yuca* cussed.

---

[267] Shut your mouth.

[268] You are too old.

[269] You should retire.

[270] Who is this ox?

[271] You better be good, ox, or you are gonna blow.

[272] Who brought this ox?

[273] Shut up damn Leona. Live that boy alone.

[274] Don't get involved damn yuca.

[275] If you continue to bother 1 will break your mother, damned pothead..

[276] Damned useless over-sized body.

La Leona moved to the back of the bus, mumbling obscenities. He lay down across two seats to sleep. *La Yuca* curled up on his seat as he told me not to worry about *la Leona*. *He* was just a loud mouthed bully but he was also a good friend.

The first month of lettuce harvest was in Welton, Arizona. It was followed by four months in Imperial Valley and one last month back in Welton. It was a daily two hundred and forty mile, round-trip but, the people were eager and willing to make the sacrifice after the long summer. On my first day of work I was assigned to form a *trio* with *La Yuca*. It was a partnership that lasted for many years and we developed a great friendship and later became *compas*[277]. The crew was slow at the start, cutting and packing with the best quality possible. It was a successful strategy. The company was famous for harvesting quality lettuce, packed carefully to give the boxes a good presentation during the mornings. This was a good strategy to lured buyers to place large orders. The more boxes the company sold, the more money the workers earned. In the afternoon when most companies were going home, *los Saikoneros* continued working until sundown to complete the orders. During the morning the crew engaged in conversations about current events or sports. There was the usual teasing and harassing of one another. By midmorning and throughout the rest of the day the passiveness of the crew disappeared and a fierce competition between *trios* began. It became a cutting and packing competition. The winners boasted all day about their superiority. The losers became the target of cruel remarks. At the end of the day, everyone was exhausted and dragging their feet as we walked to the bus for the long trip home. In the bus, it was usually silent and occasionally moans of weary workers could be heard. Some workers would try to disguise their pain out of pride, but their expressions reflected their agony. The bus driver would take us to the closest liquor

---

[277] The Godfather of my son.

store or market to get our provisions for the long haul.

"*Párate donde diga liquor*[278]," shouted the crew as we approached the store.

Everyone got off the bus in search of his favorite drink, mostly beer and whiskey. We also bought snacks to ease the hunger. As we drove off, and with every sip of the liquor, the ambiance became lively. Suddenly, *Chencho*, an old *veterano*, pulled out a huge glass. He poured a shot of his whiskey and passed the glass to *Chon*, a *lechuguero* next to him. The glass went around the bus to everyone and returned to *Chencho* when it was full with samples of every drink available. The *veterano* took a drink and passed the glass to *Chon* and around the bus for everyone to take a shot.

"*Vieja el que no le entre*[279]," said *Chon*, challenging everyone to drink from the bizarre mixture.

"*Comenzó la hora cuchi cuchi*[280]," shouted *Chencho*, imitating a child's voice.

Dazed by the liquor and penetrated by a mixture of *grifa*[281] and cigarette smoke, the *lechugueros* transformed the interior of the bus into a *cantina*[282]. The gamblers took over the back of the bus while the rest of the crew engaged in a variety show. *Chencho* and *Chon* formed a formidable comic show throughout the journey. They had good enough repertoires to tease and joke everyone in the crew. The main event was a duel of *lechugueros* imitating popular, Mexican singers. *La hora cuchi cuchi* ended upon arrival and amidst the threats of the foreman to pick up the trash and to stay sober enough to work the next day. The daily crew

---

[278] Stop where it says liquor.

[279] Phrase meaning: Anyone who doesn't dare is a broad.

[280] The happy hour has begun.

[281] Marihuana.

[282] Bar

activity repeated itself throughout the years. We were the third of four crews with similar routines. On early release days the crew leaders would challenge each other with a baseball game. It was as an extension of *la hora cuchi cuchi*. For a while, we were relieved from the hardships of the *lechuguero* life. *Los Saikoneros* endured abuses on a daily basis. Workers were expected to work under extreme conditions with little or no rest. They were subject to the lowest rate of pay in the valley. The restrooms were filthy and the water was usually undrinkable. The foremen treated the people with arrogance and looked for ways to humiliate the workers. Favoritism for the workers who kissed up to the foremen was obvious. Many *veteranos*[283] made the foremen *compadres*[284] to enjoy privileges.

The crews were formed by seniority rules placing the older *veteranos* in the first two crews. They were the most loyal workers. They had been exposed to enslaving practices before and the abuses by the foremen seemed normal. Our crew was formed by younger *lechugueros* and we were free spoken. I was the youngest when I started at age seventeen. We did not like the treatment but stayed because of the economic need. The general consensus was that if you did not like it, you could look for work somewhere else. *Los Saikoneros* developed resiliency throughout the years and formed a legacy of tough *lechugueros*.

"*Hola compañeros*[285]," said a tall, black man as he approached us.

He was member of *La Unión de Campesinos*[286] and was out recruiting workers to organize the upcoming union elections. *Mochombo, Memo* and I had been isolated from the crew to work in a small corner of the field. The black man explained that he had tried to speak to the other workers in the main crew but everyone refused to speak, intimidated

---

[283] Veterans

[284] It is the Godfather of ones child.

[285] Hello partners.

[286] Farm Workers Union

by the presence of the foremen. Without any pressure, we listened to the man with interest. There had been an ongoing campaign for a few years to unionize farm labor. We had already been under contract with the Teamsters Union for a couple of years. We had enjoyed some benefits such as salary increase, and medical insurance. Now the state laws were allowing other unions to participate in an election. Workers were given the opportunity to elect a union. The candidates were: The Teamsters, an independent union and The United Farm Workers Union. The companies rejected the idea of having a union. Some tolerated the Teamsters but they all rejected *la Unión de Campesinos de Cesar Chávez*[287].

The next day the tall black man, accompanied by another man, knocked on my door. María Elena looked out the window to see who it was.

"What do they want?" asked María Elena with concern.

"I don't know. They are *Chavistas*," I said.

"Don't get involved," said María Elena. "It is too dangerous," she cautioned.

"They are trying to help us," I said.

María Elena was not supportive of my participation with the union.

I invited the two men inside and we spoke for a few minutes. They invited me to the union office the next day after work to begin planning for the campaign. I joined la *Union de Campesinos* to help organize Crew Three of the *Saikoneros*. The four crews had an organizer but only Crew Three and Four were strong supporters of *la causa*. Crew One and Two were full of *veteranos* who had strong ties and sympathized with the company. It took persistence to get their support. But the majority of *los Saikoneros* were craving change. The younger workers were eager to confront the company and do whatever was needed to get a contract.

---

[287] Cesar Chavez's Farm workers Union.

We formed a strong negotiating team. Jesus, *Mochombo*, *Memo* and I represented the four crews in the negotiation meetings. The sessions were heated. The company negotiators tried to intimidate us by raising their voices with harsh remarks. They tried to confuse us with their lawyer talk. But, despite our illiteracy, we defended our positions well. Jesus and I were English fluent and we served as interpreters for the state lawyers. We did better than the regular interpreters because we were well-versed with farm working terms and the way farm workers talk. Our negotiating team had a strong personality and we were not intimidated by the presence of *el patron*[288].

The first election campaign was successful. Sun Harvest was the first company to sign a contract for *la Union de Campesinos*. It was the largest company with thousands of worker's. They set an important precedent for other companies. Only two large companies won the elections to maintain themselves free of unions: Bud Antle and Bruce Church. These companies doubled the wages to get the workers support. For the companies who voted for *la Unión de Campesinos*, contracts were negotiated independently. Our company was the largest in the valley and put up strong resistance. We had to walk out for three days to pressure the contract signature. The union contracts brought about a farm labor reform. The work practices were dignified. The interactions between foremen and workers were respectful. The restrooms were clean and the water drinkable. There were fifteen-minute breaks every two hours and a half hour lunch. The workers had medical insurance, paid vacation, and a salary increase. We enjoyed two years of prosperity.

After two years of contract, negotiations for a second term began. This time things did not go as well. During the first negotiations, the companies were isolated and pressured to sign the contracts with boycott, and walkouts. Negotiating companies did not want to have a

---

[288] The boss.

work stoppage while the competitor continued to work. The companies were rivals and benefited from each other's setbacks. In the second negotiations, the union strategy was to consolidate the contracts. The union's strategy forced all the companies to join resources, creating an invincible contender. Jesus and I argued with the other heads of companies, but, Sun Harvest was a strong supporter of having one contract. When a measure was put on the table for voting, their decision was unchallenged. They had more votes than all the other companies combined. But it was a bad idea. Resentment between the workers and the companies had increased. The companies resented the sabotage by many employees. Vengeful workers worked slowly and sloppily, hurting the production of the companies. *Los Saikoneros* thought differently; we continued with the same quality of work to keep the company competitive.

"*Esos gueyes están matando la gallina de los huevos de oro*[289]," said the *Saikoneros.*

This ideology caused resentment between the other companies' *lechugueros* and us. In the union meetings we were accused of being sellouts. Jesus and I defended our point of view and debated against the decision to unite all the companies. The companies did not want to bargain and resisted our requests from the start. They made the bargaining sessions a joke and threatened to stand together against the strike. *Los Chavistas* voted to strike almost unanimously. The general consensus was that the companies would settle right away. But the companies had decided to fight it out until the end. The first two weeks of strike went peacefully and people treated it like a picnic. But soon the workers began to lose their patience and their money. Now many more people realized that the negotiations were not going to be as easy

---

[289] These oxen are killing the hen with the golden eggs.

as everyone had expected. Now, we were facing a real struggle. Some workers abandoned the picket lines and moved to other areas to work. Some betrayed the movement and returned to work with their companies. The companies also brought workers from other areas that were willing to break the strike for money. There were many scuffles between *los esquiroles y los huelguistas*[290]. The local police agencies were not sufficient to neutralize the violence and reinforcements from neighboring counties were brought in to assist. The entire Imperial Valley became a war zone. The confrontations with police were constant. People threw rocks in response to tear gas and there were many arrests on a daily basis. *Los esquiroles* began to arm themselves and flash their guns, threatening *los huelguistas*. We were very concerned for the safety of our *lechugeros* and we advised them to be careful. All the picketed sites had violent confrontations, but we remained calm. *Los Saikoneros* maintained their peaceful protest despite a constant criticism. Our picket lines were isolated from the conflicts since we were on opposite sides of the valley. But after one excessively violent confrontation, other *huelgistas* came to our site to instigate our *lechugueros* to fight.

"*Ora pinchis coyones. Nosotros le dimos en la madre a los esquiroles y ustedes aquí con los brazos cruzados. ¡Cobardes!*[291]" shouted the instigators from their car.

Some of *los Saikoneros* were angered by the accusations and demanded action from everyone. The leader of the picket line pleaded with the angry mob to be calm. But they refused to listen and proceeded to invade the fields, threatening the scabs.

"*Vamos a darles en la madre*[292]," shouted the angry mob.

---

[290] The scabs and the strikers.

[291] Hey damned scaredy cats. We jus beat the mother out of those scabs and here you are with your arms crossed. Cowards!

[292] Let's beat the mother out of them.

Then, our worse fear came true: as the *Saikoneros* invaded the field, they were received with a rain of bullets from three *esquiroles*. One of the bullets hit *Rufino* in the head, killing him instantly. The news spread like fire throughout the valley and people from everywhere gathered at the union grounds to mourn our martyr.

Rufino's death brought the strike to a halt. Many celebrities, including Cesar Chavez and Governor Brown, came to his funeral. Over ten thousand mourners marched behind the funeral procession to his final resting place in the Calexico's Cemetery. We knew the strike was lost. The attempts to continue with the picket lines were in vain. Many *huelguistas* became disillusioned and scared by the events abandoned the strike. *Los Saikoneros* disbanded in many directions. They searched for refuge in other companies. At first it was hard to get a job, since we were black balled for our participation in the strike. Our reputation as instigators made us undesirable. The costly struggle to retain our benefits had failed. We lost a good friend and the abuse in the fields was more severe than ever. The wages went down and the treatment towards the workers was harsh. We lost our seniority and the hope of ever organizing again. The fields became an undesirable place to work. Los Saikoneros lost the stability and the family environment they had enjoyed. We wandered in small bands from one company to the other trying to recreate the friendly atmosphere we once had. But as the years went by, the legacy of *los Saikoneros* faded away.

EL WELFERERO

MY FAMILY'S RETURN FROM Guadalajara was relieving. I longed for
Maria Elena's cooking. I missed the kids: their laughter, shouting and
mischievousness. I missed my fights and reconciliations with María
Elena. My financial situation was very critical. I had to look for assistance
somewhere else since Workman's Compensation continued to detain my
benefits. I could not wait for their decision any longer and I was not
going to be forced to return to work in my condition. I had always been
a survivor, searching for ways to alleviate my problems. The simplest
solution for this problem was to seek public assistance and become a
welferero[293]. María Elena and I agreed to apply for welfare. We had
used public assistance before to survive the harsh summers. The routine
was to work hard during the winter to save money and build up my
unemployment benefits. When work was scarce, we applied for available
assistance programs. With four children and my meager earnings, we
qualified for all.

We had survived a long period of extreme living conditions. For
eleven years we lived in a small, run-down, one bedroom apartment. It

---

[293] Welfare recipient.

had a small storage room where our children crowded to sleep. We had a constant battle with all kinds of pests. The apartment was built on a raised floor, providing the perfect environment for roaches, spiders, and mice. We endured many harsh summers without air conditioning. We used an old water cooler that blew warm air. When the heat was unbearable we would jump into small, plastic pools to cool off under the shade of a large tree. The winter was just as bad, with cold winds blowing through the old, cracked walls which caused frigid conditions inside the apartment. We all slept wearing several layers of clothing. We moved in when we had our first born. It was to be a temporary stay and we were thinking of moving later to a larger place. But, we never did. Jose and Albert were born later, making it more difficult to fit in the small apartment. We talked about looking for a larger house but we could not find affordable ones. The unstable wages in the fields were not enough to meet the expenses. María Elena offered to work, but I always rejected that idea. I did not want her to work in the fields like our mothers. Besides, despite the degrading living conditions, I felt at peace. It was the same way I had lived for years with my parents. I resigned myself to living with what I had.

"*Con que hayga pa tragar*[294]," I would say.

I lamented my situation, but I did not have the ambition to change my way of life.

As the years went by, the conditions of the apartment deteriorated and life there became unbearable. Maria Elena's tolerance was overwhelmed and she complained often. She urged me to get another place to live. I tried to give her the same excuses as before but she refuted them. She became relentless. María Elena's greatest desire was to have her own home and she constantly encouraged me to find a way to make it true. We would talk about it and make plans. But if getting a better

---

[294] As long as there is something to eat.

apartment was difficult for me, buying a home was next to impossible. A monthly payment for a house was more than I earned in a month. The thousands of dollars needed for the down payment were out of my reach. My parents and some friends had obtained their homes through programs for low-income families. We had applied, but we did not qualify because we were a young family. We only had one child and needed at least two, to qualify. By the time we had our second child the housing projects were at a stand still. The economy was in a slump and the government was not subsidizing any low-income, home programs. We had to wait a few years for new projects to start. There were many informational meetings to arouse interest. The meetings brought hope for many families. There were five hundred families competing for fifty homes. I was reluctant to go because the funds for the project had not been approved yet. The meetings were usually disorderedly and heated arguments about who would get the houses were frequent. Conflicts were instigated by relatives and friends of the organizers, who claimed they had priority over the rest of the people. I hated to go and listen to the arguments, but María Elena always convinced me.

"If we don't attend the meetings, we will never know if we qualify," she insisted.

Six years went by and the hope of getting a home vanished for many people. But not for María Elena, who persistently acquire fresh information about the homes. She heard a rumor about letters that were sent to families that had applied. We had not received one and María Elena became very concerned. She wanted to question why we had been excluded. I tried to reason with her that we probably had not qualified because there were so many families to choose from.

"The homes are for the relatives and friends of the organizers," I told María Elena.

I always thought that it was a corrupt program and the families that really needed the homes would be excluded. But, María Elena had faith that representatives of the state would take the final decision and we could prevail against the recommendations of the local organizers. Once again she convinced me to go and again, I reluctantly accompanied her to the Farmer's Home Administration offices. We went to the office very early. They had just opened and the office was empty when we first arrived. We approached the secretary who looked up and greeted us.

"We come to get information on the new homes," María Elena said to the secretary.

"Did you get a letter confirming your application?" asked the secretary.

"Yes," María Elena lied.

When the secretary asked for the letter, María Elena said she had lost it. But the secretary could not find our records because they had not sent us a confirmation letter. She tried to dismiss us, but María Elena insisted that we had applied. The secretary went into an office to consult with a man who came out to speak to us.

"They came to apply for a home but they don't have a confirmation letter," explained the secretary.

"It is OK," said the agent. "If they know about us it is probably because they received the letter. Put them on the list," he added.

The man looked at us and smiled.

"You are the first ones to reply to the letter. First come, first serve," he said. "I will give you an appointment for tomorrow. If you bring all the information you need, you will be one of the first families to get a house," he concluded.

We left the office very excited. We could not believe our good fortune. María Elena's persistence had paid off. All of our documents were in order. We had been very careful to keep our application and required documents updated in anticipation of this moment. We returned the next day for our appointment. By this time the office was crowded with people trying to submit their applications. The state agents conducted a fair process, promptly dismissing all discrepancies created by the local organizers. Within a few weeks they distributed the houses to a few deserving families that qualified.

"Lucio! They called!" gasped María Elena.

She hugged and kissed me with excitement as I came in the house from work. She dragged me to the next room and sat on the sofa and she cuddled in my arms.

"They called," she repeated.

"Who called?" I asked.

"Farmer's Home Administration. They asked if we were still interested in a house and gave us an appointment to sign an agreement this afternoon," she said.

That afternoon we went and signed the contract. We had qualified to get our house. Our miracle had just come true. The house was in the final stages of completion. It would take a couple of weeks before we could move in, but they gave us access to the house. We went to visit our house daily. We spend most of the day there. María Elena was planning the decorations while I cultivated the yard for our future garden. The kids chose their rooms. Jose and Alberto would share one room while Lucio would get the other one. They had plenty of space to run about inside and outside the house. It was hard to return to the old apartment after spending many hours in the new house. Alberto would complain and resisted the return. He always questioned why we could not stay. María Elena and the children complained about a nasty odor in the apartment. The bad smell came from an old drainpipe leaking under the floor of the apartment. It became more eminent after we spent a few hours smelling the odors of the new house. The sudden stink in the old shack was disgusting. The heat was unbearable. After spending a few hours in the cool climate provided by the new air conditioner, no one wanted to return to the old cooler blowing hot air. The last few nights we spent there were nightmares. We could not wait to move out and start a new life.

Our living conditions improved dramatically in our new home. We moved from a run-down, infested shack to a beautiful three-bedroom palace. The house had a beautiful kitchen with cabinets and a new stove. The large, carpeted living room had a window looking out the front yard. Outside, the house had a large front and back yard. We had plenty of room to garden and built a barbecue, and plenty of space for the kids to play. Amazingly, we had moved in without having to give a down payment. The monthly installment was based on our income. We only paid twenty five percent of the actual monthly payment. Our friends envied our good fortune. They sarcastically called us *los ricos pobres*[295] because we lived in homes we could not afford without the government assistance.

I became very skilled at searching local assistance programs. I was very persistent at meeting the requirements and bringing in plenty of resources for my family. I became cocky and bragged about my skills to my friends.

"*No nomás es vivir, hay que saber vivir*[296]," I would say to them.

My friends admired my strategies and my relentlessness.

"*No saben que chinche se echaron en su petate*[297]," they teased. Through the harsh years I had acquired a productive sense of cunning to improve my situation. I was learning to use my disadvantages to benefit my family. For some people having a large family was seen as a burden; for *welfereros* it was a blessing.

---

[295] The rich poor.

[296] It is not just living, you have to learn how to live.

[297] They don't know the kind of flea they have in their mat.

Our fourth baby was born in the first year living in our home. At first, I was reluctant to have another baby. I later changed my mind, influenced by a popular consensus in our neighborhood that the more family one has, the more assistance one receives. Besides, María Elena had longed for a daughter. She was the only female in the house and she missed the company of a girl. But her wish was not to be. Instead we got our fourth son, Miguel Angel. We were not the only ones having a baby in the neighborhood; fifteen children were born in the first year in our block alone. Ironically, by having many children, the future of low-income families improved. The more children a family had the more benefits they would receive.

Our appointment at the welfare department went very well. Our social worker was very sympathetic. She could not believe that the insurance was denying my benefits despite my injury. After arranging emergency assistance, the social worker went out the office to contact the insurance. After a few minutes she returned.

"I called them. If you don't receive a check with all your back pay this week, come back and let me know," the social worker said.

We went home relieved, knowing that we would be able to pay our bills and provide for our children. The welfare department would provide money, food stamps, and medical aid to alleviate our basic needs. In addition, they would pressure Workman's Compensation to provide my benefits. Within a few days I received my first Workman's Compensation check. With this assistance, our level of life returned to normal.

THE AWAKENING

As THE MONTHS WENT by, the pain in my leg decreased. The leg was still numb and crippled. I still was not able to work. My doctor said that I would never recover completely, but that the injury would heal with time if I took good care of it. He advised me to look for other types of jobs.

"You will never be a *lechuguero* again, but with time, you will be able to work in less physical jobs," he said.

My acquaintances advised me otherwise. They encouraged me to get a lawyer and demand compensation.

"*Que te paguen una feria, guey*[298]," they said.

Many stories were told of workers with injuries getting many thousands of dollars in compensation. Some people said that all they had to do was file, sue, and wait patiently for the outcome. The injured workers insisted that they could not perform any kind of work and received benefits for months until a settlement was arranged. The workers would get monetary compensation and reabilitation. Based on my *welferero* tendencies, these proposals were very appealing and I

---

[298] Let them pay you some money, ox.

made plans to take advantage of my situation. I hired an attorney and filed a claim for compensation. The process went on for months. In the mean time I sat idle around the house, waiting for all the money people said I would get. It was a monotonous routine. I would get up in the morning, prepare myself coffee, and visit my garden. I would stay in the garden for a couple of hours doing some exercises for my leg. Later in the day, I would help María Elena with some of the house chores and prepare food for lunch and dinner. Most of the day, I would sit and watch television. I became familiar with all the programs at all hours of the day. On some occasions, a visit from one of my friends, Juan, would break the repetitive routine. We would drink beer and exchange gardening tips. After a few months of this tedious routine, I began to get bored and questioned how long I would live this way. I had always been very active. I tried to look for things to do, but my lawyer discouraged me. He insisted that by staying inactive I would have a better chance of getting a large compensation. But I was not happy. I became restless. My crippled leg demoralized me and I missed my *lechuguero* environment. I missed my physical and social activities. I began to see my house as a prison. My activities were limited by the concern that the insurance would record evidence against my disability case.

My massage therapist, Ramon, who was a blind man, inspired me to overcome my injury. He said that my condition was not so serious. The Sciatic nerve was stuck in one of my Lumbar vertebrates and it could be freed with a consistent exercise routine. Ramon was very inspirational; despite his disability he carried on a very productive life. He would tease my lamenting.

"*¿Que pasa? ¿Tan poco aguantas? Te quejas por que estas renco. Yo estoy ciego y vivo muy a gusto*[299]," Ramon would say.

---

[299] What's wrong? You can't take it? You complain because you are crippled. I am blind and I live happily.

Ramon had his own business and employed several blind massage therapists. He encouraged them to be independent and productive despite their disability. I learned from him not to feel sorry for myself and to look at my setbacks as the foundation for my success. He talked to me about all the obstacles he had overcome, how he had changed to a positive individual. He made jokes about being blind. It was his shield against cruelty toward disadvantaged people. Ramon talked about nurturing our character from the pessimism of people around us. He used his determination to combat degradation.

"Entre mas te rebajen, mas la determinación de demostrar que están mal[300]," Ramon would say.

For many restless nights I went over Ramon's conversations. I was influenced by his motivating approach which empowered me to be positive. He said positive thinking was the first step in the process of change. I needed to believe in myself, that I could accomplish more and better things in my life. I wanted to learn to live by Ramon's advice.

It was difficult to change my lifestyle. It was addictive; a one way street with no return. I was not sure where to start. Ramon said that starting was the most difficult part in any task, but that once something was started many options would begin to unfold.

"I could start by overcoming my handicap," I thought to myself.

To keep myself active I would seek refuge in my garden. I loved to read about organic gardening. I learned the art and created for María Elena a wonderful garden. The flowers were beautiful and the vegetables and fruits plenty. In the garden I cared for Mikey while María Elena did her chores. Mikey was two years old and became very attached to me. We spent a lot of time together. He mimicked everything I did. He would pretend to garden and wanted to be a participant. He loved

---

[300] The more people put you down, the more determine you become to prove them wrong.

eating the vegetables and fruits we planted, especially the tomatoes and sweet peas.

"*¿Ya te fijaste que el Mikey manquea[301]?*" asked María Elena.

Just as he copied how I gardened and exercised, he began to walk with a limp. María Elena humorously urged me to walk straight.

"If you don't heal fast, Mikey will become crippled, too" she teased.

It was María Elena's humorous way to cheer me up. She always expressed her faith in my recovery.

"*Te vas aliviar pronto, ya veras[302],*" she would say.

I devoted myself to an exercise routine given to me by my doctor. I would lie on the floor and raise my legs on a pillow. As I lay, I would slowly raise my knee to my chest and hold while I pressed my spine to the floor. I alternated each leg in several repetitions throughout the day. The objective was to have the spine straight while pulling the leg muscle to wiggle the nerve loose. I became interested in that logic and began to read related books. As I began to understand my injury, the exercise became more significant. I saw the logic in pulling the muscle to ease it out. I developed the proper form in my exercise and when I pulled the muscle I could sense it moving. I learned different ways of stretching. I concentrated on pulling the leg muscles as I meditated and envisioned the nerve movement gradually becoming loose. I was devoted to my exercise routine. I repeated it at all times of the day. On one occasion, just as suddenly as the injury happened, I felt the nerve loosen. It was a great relief to feel sensation running down my leg once again. I ran to María Elena to tell her about my changing condition.

"Mikey will not be crippled after all," I said.

She looked at me puzzled and then she smiled.

"I don't understand," she said.

---

[301] Did you notice that Mickey limps?

[302] You will heal soon, you will see.

I explained how I had felt the muscle move, releasing a sensation down my leg. My lifeless toes began to recover their sense of feeling and within two days, I was able to wiggle them. Within weeks, I was able to walk without a limp. It was the greatest feeling of success I had ever felt in my life. I had learned to survive and overcome a difficult stage in my life. Perhaps this was the turning point.

"There are some openings in the district," Mr. Belcher said.

"All right!" I said.

"All right, what?" he asked, puzzled by my reply.

For many years he had proposed a variety of job alternatives, but I had always ignored him.

"Thank you for telling me; I am interested," I said.

"I never thought I would here you say that," said Mr. Belcher.

He had always told me that I deserved other opportunities to prove myself and pointed out the district as a good starting point.

"It's still labor. It's just less strenuous and has more future than the fields," Mr. Belcher said.

My doctor agreed with Mr. Belcher's proposal and compared the benefits of my two options.

"My lawyer says that if I apply for this job, it will hurt my case," I said.

The doctor was not optimistic about the insurance benefits.

"You will get some money and training for a job with no future. On the other hand, if you obtained a position in the school district your options will increase," the doctor said.

My lawyer tried to influence my decision of applying for a job. He explained that it meant deserting the case and losing the monetary compensation. Despite the risk, I became determined to look for another way. I applied for a custodial position advertised by the district. The secretary gave me the application and an appointment to take a written exam. They wanted to know how much the applicants knew about the job duties. I was ignorant on the topic and had no idea what to expect on the test. I asked Mr. Belcher for advice. He referred me to a library section containing practice books for many governmental positions. I checked out a custodial test practice book. I studied hard and passed the test, ranking number one. I went to my first interview with enthusiasm. I knew that there were others with advantages. Some applicants had experience and had worked in the district before.

"What do I have to lose? I am already at the bottom. I can't go any lower," I thought.

I gave it my best try but, I was not chosen for the job. Mr. Belcher encouraged me to apply for other positions.

"Don't give up now," he said.

I went back to the library and made a list of the books for all the governmental jobs available. I went to the district office and asked for a list of the classified positions in the district and applied for ten jobs.

"You really want to work in this district," said the secretary.

"Yes! Just leave a small opening and I will get in," I told the secretary.

I went back to the library and checked out a book for each position I applied for and prepared myself for the tests. One by one, I passed them and waited for an opportunity to interview. Since I was on the waiting list, I was offered a temporary position for the summer in the maintenance department. It was the first opportunity I had to show my skills. On my first day of work, I was assigned to paint the parking lots' lines. I was teamed with a man named David. We were part of a twelve-man crew of temporary workers waiting for a chance to land a permanent job in the district. As I learned my way around, I noticed the same behavior pattern I had experienced in the fields. The relationship between workers and management was unstable. The workers complained of unfair labor practices and dragged their feet on every assignment showing their discontent. Management, on their part, dealt with the workers with arrogance and a sense of superiority. The workers had the protection of their union, which balanced the situation but did not improve the relationship. Each side constantly complained about the other. I ignored their behavior and engulfed myself in working my way into the district. I always worked hard despite the protests of my peers, who accused me of kissing up to the boss. They wanted me to drag my feet in sorority with them. All I wanted was a job, and I was not going to get it by performing less than my capability. Besides, not only did I want a job, I wanted to be the best worker. Just like I wanted to be the best "*lechuguero*" while working in the fields, now I wanted to excel on any task I was given.

My first permanent position was as a teacher assistant in the vocational program. It was a six-hour job with benefits and decent wages. I earned my job working hard. I was a good candidate because of my experience in auto mechanics, woodwork, welding, and gardening. But the teachers greeted me with resentment because I was selected instead of their preference. I began to experience the harsh treatment other workers complained about. The teachers were arrogant and degraded me from the first moment we met. The vice-principal showed me around the campus and introduced me to the four teachers I would assist in their respective order.

"This is your new assistant," said the female administrator to the first teacher.

"Nice to meet you," I said.

I offered to shake hands, but the teacher ignored my extended hand.

"Is this guy qualified?" asked the teacher.

"He was selected in the interview," answered the administrator.

"I have experience as an auto mechanic," I said.

I was trying to gain the sympathy of the teacher by outlining the skills I had in his field. He ignored my remark and continued with his protest with the administrator.

"If he makes one mistake, I want him out of my class," the teacher concluded.

The teacher walked away. The administrator looked at me and smiled dismissing the teacher's attitude. She led me to the other teacher who was not as arrogant and rather sympathetic. He was the landscaping teacher and was glad to have someone with my gardening skills. I felt welcomed and relieved in his class. I perceived a hostile environment in the other three classrooms. It was a relief to know that I would spend half my day doing landscaping.

As we walked to the office, the administrator pointed to a building.

"That is the lounge. You have two fifteen minute breaks during your working hours. You can relax and have a snack there," she said.

After completing all the paper work, I was sent to my first assignment. I was rotated from one class to the other every period. Before going to class, I went to the lounge to take a look. I met a teacher in the walkway.

"Good morning sir," I said.

"What's so good about it?" the teacher sneered.

"Well, the weather is nice," I said.

He looked away mumbling and walked inside the lounge. I hesitated for a few seconds, and then I walked into the lounge. The grumpy teacher was sitting on a couch pretending to read a newspaper. He looked up as he saw me enter.

"What the hell are you doing here?" he barked.

"I come here to take my break," I said.

"This lounge is just for teachers," he said.

"I am a teacher assistant," I said.

"I said for teachers! Are you deaf?" he shouted.

The teacher got up and stormed out, disgusted.

"I will complain. I will not share my lounge with other employees," he mumbled.

I was startled. I never expected this kind of reception in this environment. I saw it happening in the fields, but here in a school it was disappointing. During my tenure in this job, I kept a low profile. I did my work and stayed away from other people's business. I focused on the students and only addressed the teachers to greet them or to follow their directions. I developed a rapport with the students and taught them as much as I knew. I had plenty of knowledge in all the subjects to assist them. The students trusted me and considered me a teacher. I was sympathetic to their needs. I could relate to them. They would speak well of me despite all the teachers' putdowns, causing arguments between them.

"Mr. Padilla is the best teacher. He knows more than you," said an angry student.

"He is not a teacher. He doesn't have a credential. What he knows is worthless. He is just an assistant," snapped the teacher.

The argument had developed out of the frustration of the student who could not understand a concept. With arrogance and a lack of sensibility, the teacher dismissed the student. Some of the students needed attention and more support. When they sought it, they were rejected. The disadvantaged students were always accused of being lazy or apathetic. I had inadvertently listened to the cruel statements directed at me from outside the door. I heard the commotion as I was coming in and stopped at the entrance. I walked in the class startling the teacher, who angrily walked away. I contained myself and ignored the comments. I put on my overall and proceeded to interact with the students. The situation was becoming unbearable. I tried to ignore the teacher's attitude and concentrated on my work. Later in the period, the teacher approached me and gave a directive to take the students to a meeting. I immediately carried on the order. I was glad I was leaving the class. The meeting turned out to be orientation for the community college. Many students were fidgeting uninterested, but the information caught my attention. Mr. Aragón, the college counselor, was very inspirational. He had been a custodian who worked himself through school. He spoke to students about the importance of an education and all the opportunities everyone had to attain it. Mr. Aragón explained the educational and financial services available at the community college for those who were willing to make the effort.

"There are no excuses. Everyone has the opportunity to continue school," Mr. Aragón said.

As the counselor spoke, the words of the arrogant teacher repeated in my head.

"He doesn't have a credential. He is worthless," the teacher had said.

The remarks from the teacher had upset me. But now, after listening to Mr. Aragón, I realized that I was at fault. The lack of initiative, direction, and determination provoked the criticism. I had always excused myself by blaming my hardships for my disadvantages. I had consistently disregarded positive observations and recommendations. Mr. Belcher had always encouraged me to better my situation. He had shown his sympathy for my drawbacks and offered me good advice which I ignored. The critics did not understand or care for my shortcomings. They pointed out my lack of ambition. They perceive me as lazy and a burden to society, a second class citizen. It was up to me to turn their negative perceptions into constructive criticism. Perhaps I could turn their arrogance into motivation to better myself just to prove them wrong. Just like Ramón had advised.

"*Entre mas me rebajen, mas les demuestro que están mal*[303]," I thought.

I could interpret their cruel, degrading remarks and use them as inspiration. Their humiliation could be the key to awaken me from this long-lasting trance I was in.

---

[303] The more they degrade me the more I show them wrong.

RETURN TO ROCKWOOD

I DID NOT LAST long as a teacher assistant. I liked to work with the students but it was only a part time job, the environment was hostile, and the salary was one of the lowest in the district. I promptly applied for the position of grounds keeper at Rockwood Elementary, a full time position with benefits and opportunities to work overtime. I knew I could excel as a gardener. The position was vacated by Ted, one of the few Anglo employees in the district. He had given me the impression that he was lethargic because of the condition of his school. He gained my respect when I found out he had just obtained his teaching credential. Ted was setting the example for the rest of the classified employees to improve their status.

"I can be the second maintenance worker to get a credential," I thought to myself.

Taking over his position motivated me to follow his example. The tool room was full of evidence of his trajectory. The walls were full of posters with inspirational messages.

"If you think education is expensive, try ignorance," read one poster.

This message caught my attention because I could relate to it. All my life I had already tried ignorance and I had paid the consequences.

"Now it is was my turn to try education," I thought.

Rockwood's ambience was just right to thrive in. The school had just gone through reconstruction and the grounds were completely destroyed. I had the opportunity to show my skills rebuilding the playgrounds. Teachers were friendly and motivated. They welcomed me and praised my innovations. I also had support from Mrs. Wilkerson, the school principal. She approved the ground's renovation plan and encouraged my quest for an education. The greatest inspiration came from the memories I had as a student at Rockwood. It was the first school I attended when I crossed the border. Now, I had a chance to contribute and show my appreciation for the things I learned.

I had many memorable moments while working at Rockwood School. I started a vegetable garden project where all the students were involved. Each class had a four by fourteen feet plot to grow seasonal vegetables and flowers. I would prepare the soil during the summer and the students would plant and care for the plots under my supervision throughout the school year. Teachers made lesson plans to incorporate the gardens with their science and language arts lessons. The students would plant, grow, and eat carrots, broccoli, cauliflower, cabbage, tomatoes, and sweet peas. The classes competed to see who would grow the larges strawberry. The prize would be an array of vegetables with their favorite dip for the whole class. The creation of "The Green Thumb Club" gave me the opportunity to work with students. The club members were students from all grade levels and they had a variety of duties to care for the gardens. The students would proudly wear their club badge as they went about the gardens during recess. The gardens gave the students a hands on opportunity to learn to grow plants. They saw the plants develop from seed to maturity. They were able to harvest and eat the product. It was a tasty conclusion.

The garden project gave me prestige in the district. Many people showed their appreciation for my dedication. Unfortunately, it also brought resentment. Other schools began to question why Rockwood was the only school with such an activity. The other grounds keepers resisted the pressure to start their own gardens in their schools. They argued that it was not part of their job description and it took time from more important duties. The maintenance supervisor began to see my activities as a threat and they asked me to stop. I was making all the others look bad and a rivalry had developed. I was not concerned. To make a good impression in this position, I had to do things that were out of the ordinary. The more they asked me to stop, the more innovations I developed. I was able to maintain the project alive for five years until I involuntarily transferred to a skilled grounds position. It was a tactic to solve the problem. It was a better paid job, but it isolated me from the environment I was thriving in. I complained, but the supervisor argued that I was being promoted.

"We are giving you the best opportunity of your life," he said.

Perhaps for other employees this would be the opportunity of their lives. But my goals were not to be a skilled grounds keeper. My goal was to become an educator.

THE GRADUATES

I'VE NEVER HAD ANY significant goals in my life. Whenever I made plans, there was always a justification to abandon them. The two most common excuses were working an unpredictable shift and the influence of my friends. They were my main restraint. It was an addictive routine that consumed most of my times, making me neglect everything else, including my family. I made several attempts to change, but I surrendered easily. With a severe case of an inferiority complex, I functioned in the syndrome of "NO". I can't do it" was my logo. A self degrading frame of mind deeply integrated in my behavior pattern.

Education was never a priority in our family. I never ventured into anything outside my established routine. I was not expected to learn a trade or make a career. Our parents were illiterate. No one in my family had experienced higher education in the United States. Only María Elena's brother, Roberto, had gone to an American university through a military fund. Roberto and his wife had careers; he was a laboratory technician in a military hospital and she was an elementary school teacher. Ironically, when we told them that María Elena and I were going to school, they ridiculed us.

"What are you taking?" Roberto taunted.

"I am taking Liberal Studies courses," I said.

"Those classes are too difficult," Roberto's wife smirked.

"Yeah, you should take welding, auto tech, or something you can handle," Roberto said.

"I don't think you can handle teaching," Roberto's wife sneered.

They degraded us by superiority. But, I did not feel inferior anymore. Instead, I felt pity for their ignorance. Their education could not conceal their arrogance. Instead of using their successful experience to motivate us, Roberto and his wife treated us with contempt, an action that strengthened my pride. The remarks would have discouraged me before. But now, I was devoted to breaking the illiterate chain that held down our family.

The local community college offered an opportunity for people with disadvantages like me. Many of the students were facing the same challenges. They came from uneducated and underprivileged families, attempting to break away apathetic trend towards education. The careers to pursue were limited, but academically challenging. The college offered an array of remedial classes to prepare deficient students to meet the requirements. It also administered the General Education Development test, or GED, for students like me who had not completed high school. An efficient financial aid program alleviated the financial burden of many students. The opportunity was there. The only missing element was the commitment to face the demanding workload. The start of the semester was enthusiastic; the classes were full. But, by mid-semester, the dropout rate was enormous. The trial was not easy. Dropouts had their constraints. The young students lacked academic skills and had not yet experienced the hardships of life to make the effort. The older students had families and jobs that interfered with their attendance. It was a clear display of the syndrome of "NO" I can't do it." The demanding workload was demoralizing to those who were not fully committed. They always had a good excuse to drop out. My devotion to learn was beyond any constraints. I was ready. I was tired of the hardships of life. I was ready to sacrifice myself.

I adapted well to college. The environment was friendly. The students were common people, just like me. I could learn just as well as them. My general knowledge was vast due to my inclination for reading, which gave me an edge in most classes. My desire, hard work, and dedication placed me at the top of all my classes. My assignments were my priority during my daily routine. It was important to maintain a high grade average to qualify for financial assistance and to compete for student grants. They were crucial to help cover the cost of school.

The following year, our oldest son Lucio graduated from high school and enrolled in the Liberal Studies Program. He was the eldest. María Elena and I wanted him to set the example for his three younger brothers. Lucio had his own motivations and challenges. He had the wisdom to mend his mistakes. Best of all, Lucio learned to appreciate education during his high school years. Early on, he set high goals for himself. Lucio was a teenager in search of his identity and his independence. His decisions were difficult because of the abundance of distractions that disorient many adolescents. He had not worked in the fields but he had experienced the hardships of the farm worker's family. He had what it took to break away from uncertainty.

Lucio and I drew attention when we attended the same classes. Our age difference was only seventeen years. We looked like brothers. With the same name, address, phone number and major, we created occasional confusion. Our data was usually confused. We saved money and work by sharing books and notes. Our story came out on front page of the valley's newspaper twice, once when we graduated with a Bachelor and again a few years later with a Master's in Educational Administration. It was a great accomplishment. Lucio and I had established a precedent that would stimulate motivation in our family and others around us. We were the first graduates.

I was proud of my school performance. It was like old times when I was the best *lechuguero*, pompous after displaying my swift and efficient skills. My degree was my greatest accomplishment. I graduated with honors, Magna Cum Laude, among the best in my class. My quest for education was extensive and arduous. For many years, I was a full time student with a full time job. The work load was exhausting and time consuming. I became obsessed with the challenge. My nature was to work hard. Every moment of the day, school was on my mind. I was always planning about meeting my responsibilities. I was used to harsh physical work. But the mental effort soon began to take its toll. I became stressed-out, irritable, and arrogant. I expected everyone to work as hard as me. When someone slacked, I became confrontational. I tried to impose my will with threats and intimidation. I distanced myself from María Elena. She completed her Associate Degree and shifted her attention elsewhere. María Elena was deteriorating physically and emotionally due to the stress. In a span of five years, her father and three brothers died. Her mother was elderly and needed attention. But her biggest worries were our sons as they entered different stages of adolescence. They presented different challenges as they sought their autonomy. The volatile home environment provoked power struggles between us. My sons defied my authority and María Elena sided with them. I became bitter. Everyone was summoned to comply with my authority or suffer the consequences. I was an egotistical, constantly displaying the "My way or the highway" attitude. My family became resentful and weary of me. We fought constantly and our confrontations went without reconciliation. Healing the emotional wounds of the conflicts turned complex. I became isolated. I felt everyone was out to get me. I was always irate and rejected any intent of communication. Tired of our situation, María Elena threatened me with divorce. I was exasperated. I returned to my old ways when I was a *Saikonero* and sought refuge in *la hora cuchi cuchi*, the happy hour in which many *lechugueros* drank their sorrows away.

The chaos caused my sons to go astray. The lack of effective parenting skills and the hostility made our sons vulnerable to negative influences. The younger boys lost interest in school. They vigorously rejected our advice. Just like I had done as a teenager, they did their will. They wanted to experiment the thrills and pains of life. María Elena was feeling the anguish our mothers must have felt when we were looking for our autonomy unprepared to face up to the responsibilities. My family was deteriorating and I was desperately trying to find a culprit. I thought it was their fault. I was making a great effort to overcome our hardships and they did not show appreciation. I also wanted tranquility to enjoy my success, but I could not find it with their opposition. Unfortunately, my arrogance did not allow me to see that the answer was within me. I was still trapped in the syndrome of thinking I didn't have to change. I had managed to escape from it educationally, but I was still emotionally attached to the myths and misconceptions of what the head of family role was. Predisposed by the ignorance of my value system, I followed the only pattern I had witnessed. I was the man of the house and that was that.

PARENTING EDUCATION?

"*LEVANTEN LA MANO LOS que son padres de familia*[304]," said the teacher.

Everyone in the room raised their hands. We were confused by the question. She knew we were all parents.

"*Claro que soy padre. Por eso estoy aquí, por un cabrón chamaco que se esta portando mal*[305]," said an angry man.

A murmur spread across the room. In a second, everyone shared their perils with the person sitting next to them. We were a group of parents attending a mandated parenting class because of our children's misbehavior. I went reluctantly. I was upset and embarrassed to be there. I was a few weeks from starting my first teaching assignment and I found myself attending mandatory parenting classes. I felt that it would tarnish my reputation. I would be seen as a bad father and incompetent teacher. I was not. I had been harsh with my family but always with the intention to spare them of the hazards of life. I felt that by being strict, I would keep them safe. The teacher introduced herself and announced a ruthless schedule under the protests of the participants. The program

---

[304] Raise your hand if you are a parent.

[305] Of course I am a parent. I am here because of a damned kid who is behaving badly.

was nine weekly sessions, three-hours long. We had to complete the program or make-up any absences. The people lamented the time they were wasting.

"*En vez de estar haciendo otras cosas, aquí estoy perdiendo mi tiempo a causa de este cabrón[306]*," said the angry man.

The first activity of the class was to introduce ourselves and share a few personal facts. There were people from every social level in our community; educated people with good careers as well as farm workers and laborers. Our common ground was having a problematic child.

"*¿Quien de ustedes fue a la escuela?*" the teacher asked.

She paused momentarily. A few hands went up.

"*Para ser padres[307]*," the teacher continued.

Everyone laughed.

"*¿Cual escuela? No hay[308]*," said another parent.

¿De donde aprendieron sus estrategias de parentasgo[309]?" The teacher asked.

"*Aprendimos de nuestros padres[310]*," some parents said.

"The most important task of a human being is to be a parent, yet many parents do not prepare themselves for the task," said the teacher. "Parents commit themselves with out knowing the implications."

Everyone agreed that using what we learned from our parents is fine if the lessons were positive. Most people I knew treated their children *a madrasos y ralladas de madre[311]*. Ironically, the harsh treatment I ran away

---

[306] Instead of doing other things, here I am wasting my time because of this damned kid.

[307] To be parents.

[308] What school? There is none.

[309] Where did you learn your parenting strategies?

[310] We learned from our parents.

[311] With whippings and swearing.

from as a teen was now part of my discipline repertoire. The teacher also talked of unconditional love for our dear ones. She explained that love was the most powerful tool to bring about harmony and was the foundation for change.

"Love your children for what they are, not for what they will become," The teacher said.

"Deal with bad behavior by avoiding conflict," she said. "Treasure your family's relationship."

Our homework for the first session was to practice saying "I love you" and avoiding fighting at all costs. It had been a long time since I last used those words. They had been erased from my vocabulary by my anger. I never told my sons that I loved them. I felt awkward saying it. It had been a while since I told María Elena that I loved her even though I had vowed to do it all my life.

The teacher was a powerful presenter who captivated people with her enthusiasm. She turned her class into a nurturing environment that encouraged a conscious self analysis. We were able to seek deep inside ourselves and identify and heal the profound wounds in our family relationship. The root of the problem was within our selves. For a long time, I had waited searching elsewhere or blaming others for my mistakes. And now, in the place I least expected, I was finding the source and the solution to my problems. The class left in me a striking impression that incited change; from angry and stressed to calm and hopeful. María Elena and I talked about the class until late hours. We agreed we had to change if we wanted our sons' behavior to improve. We had to foster an appealing home environment by promoting love and affection. We had to avoid conflict and amend our blunders to heal our emotional wounds. We had to encourage and support our children's pursuit for an identity and independence to become self sufficient and productive adults. We had lost so much time. Just like I had worked hard to break the trend of apathy for school, I wanted to break the trend of indifference towards the development of my family. There were so many things to learn. The time was just as good as any to start. Just like my quest for an education, I would make the changes necessary to develop a positive relationships and to become a positive influence in my family.

María Elena and I attended every single class. We were the only couple completing the course. Most of the others were single parents or couples that alternated their attendance. The parenting classes ended one day before my first teaching assignment. The knowledge I had acquired about behavior development opened a world of new opportunities. I was able to understand many of the destructive behaviors of my students. Implementing what I had learned in the parenting trainings allowed me to provide better services for my students. My first teaching assignment was in special education. The students presented a challenge academically, socially, and emotionally. They had learning disabilities, apathy, insecurity, and hyperactivity. But the most marked deficiency was the lack of proper parenting. Some students were over protected or extremely neglected. Most parents were ignorant of the disabilities of their children and did not know how to deal with the problem.

To work with these students I had to finish a Special Education Program to get a teaching credential. The program offered classes related to learning disabilities in reading, writing, and math. But the curriculum that grabbed my attention was the behavior modification trainings. Many of the concepts were related to parenting values. I began to see the correlation and used them as character building strategies for my students. I constructed a positive environment that helped many disadvantaged children. I could relate to them and it was at my advantage to help them. My class was the breaking ground where I promoted motivating strategies. My supervisors saw my potential and offered me additional training in behavior and parenting concepts. Soon, I was one of their most active facilitators promoting effective parenting strategies.

My teaching career had a good head start. I was able to develop a rapport with my students and their parents. I encouraged them to come to our parenting trainings to learn to deal with behavior without conflict. A proper home and school environment led to significant improvement in the students' school performance. As their academic performance improved, the once rejected special education students were allowed to participate in general classes, opening new opportunities for them. I was having success and rewarding accomplishments.

While I was having success at school, at home things moved at slower pace. Initially, my children did not trust me and rejected my approach. At times I would get desperate, doubting the efficiency of the strategies I was endorsing.

"Why is it not working for me?" I questioned myself.

I was able to help others but I was not helping myself.

The severed relationship with my family slowed the process of change. Whenever we had a positive outcome, something drastic would happen and in one instant the effort of many days would go to waste. My frustration would not allow me to enjoy my family and my success. I needed peace in my mind and my soul.

"How can anybody be happy with this anxiety?" I wondered.

Stressful situations do not allow anyone to enjoy the pleasures of life. Successful careers, money, social status, and a good reputation are worthless when you lack love. It is the reason for existence: being able to care and be cared for by your family. Why start a family if we are not going to care for it? It was a question I repeated in my trainings to parents, but actually, it was directed at me. My continuing in the parenting program helped me to slowly adjust. Reviewing the concepts with other parents gave me the resolve to develop patience and tolerance, since behavior takes time to transform.

THE OLD LECHUGUERO

I AM A FORTUNATE person. I have experienced different aspects of life. I have learned to be resourceful and deal with setbacks. I make wiser decisions to accomplish the important functions of a human being. I had the resolve to heal my injury. I found the way out of a degrading ignorance that limited me for many years. I worked myself out of illiteracy and became a successful professional. But the new light of my life is the tranquility I have found in the harmony of my family. I have changed so much. I am the opposite of what I was in my youth. I was able to come to terms with myself and my dear ones. My relationship with María Elena has bloomed. We care for each other. We spend quality time traveling, shopping, or just relaxing at home. "I love you", is a common and sincere phrase in our daily conversations. María Elena is who I want to be with until the end of life. I also strengthened my relationship with my parents and siblings. I sought healing the relationship with my father. I feel internal peace for being able to tell him that I loved him before his death. The relationship with my mother, my brother and my sisters is strong. We are a united family and we have pledged to care for each other and together care for our widowed mother. I was able to influence my sister Silvia to educate herself. After many years of working in the fields, she also became a teacher. The younger ones followed the example and we became a family of educators. Despite all the disadvantages my family has experienced, we have developed a strong foundation for our future generations. My sons are auto-sufficient and economically sound. They are educationally oriented and advancing their academic goals.

Their children are being raised in a nurturing environment. Not a trace of the unenthusiastic rearing they experienced is evident in their lives. The healing process has advanced considerably. They are setting productive precedents that will influence our immediate as well as our extended family. Our dreams have come true. Our sons have developed into fine people. They are establishing strong family values. Their relationship with their wives and children is their most important asset. The nurturing environment around their children will give them the opportunity to develop to their greatest potential. María Elena and I are enjoying our latter years watching the healthy growth of our grandchildren. We are devoted to developing a strong relationship with them. We want to be trusted grandparents that will listen when they need someone to speak with. Our aspiration is that our sons and their families come and visit us in old age out of caring rather than out of responsibility. I am grateful for all I have: a stable future, a loving wife, and a beautiful family. Listening to our grand children say, *"Te quiero mucho abuelito*[312]*,"* is our joy.

---

[312] I love you so much grandfather.

It is uncertain how much I will accomplish in the years I have left to live. I will continue my advocacy for parenting programs and promote the concepts that have significantly changed my life. I am certain my children will continue with the campaign to improve education in our schools. I am convinced that our legacy will leave a clear mark in our community. As I look back at my life, I smile and say to my self, "*¿que más puede pedir un viejo lechuguero de esta vida*[313]?"

---

[313] What else can a lettuce harvester ask off this life?

CPSIA information can be obtained
at www.ICGtesting.com
Printed in the USA
FSHW011956221020
75150FS